EXTENSIONS OF AFRICAN CULTURES IN BRAZIL

EXTENSIONS OF AFRICAN CULTURES IN BRAZIL

GERHARD KUBIK

DIASPORIC AFRICA PRESS

This book is a publication of

DIASPORIC AFRICA PRESS
NEW YORK | WWW.DAFRICAPRESS.COM

Copyright © 2013 Diasporic Africa Press, Inc.

All rights reserved. No part of this publication may be reproduced or distributed in any form or by any means, or stored in a database or retrieval system, without the prior written permission of the publisher.

ISBN-13 978-1-937306-12-0 (pbk.: alk paper)
Library of Congress Control Number: 2013956650

CONTENTS

A Note on Terminology	*i*
Foreword	*iii*
Introduction	*v*
African Populations in Brazil: Cultural Group Constitution and Origins	*1*
Cultural Groupings and African-Brazilian Cultural Zones	*27*
African Language Remnants in Brazil	*67*
Dance Dramas, Popular Theater and Fighting Games	*91*
The African-Brazilian Religions: A Religious Syncretism?	*123*
On the Methodology of African-Brazilian Cultural Research	*151*
Appendix	*167*
Bibliography	*187*
Notes	*195*
Index	*201*

Map 1. Map of contemporary Brazil with 23 states, 2 national territories and one national district.

A NOTE ON TERMINOLOGY

In a work where concepts from African languages are constantly being compared with those which have been assimilated from the idiom of a European language in the Americas—such as Brazilian—the orthography of the terms must be specially treated. Cross-cultural comparisons between Brazilian and African regions are made in this book; and therefore it has proven to be of utmost importance that it is always clear to the reader what is being talked about, whether it is an African concept or an often similar-sounding and only minimally modified Brazilian concept. In order to make this discernable, we present concepts in African (or African remnant) languages in *italics* and those in African-Brazilian within quotation marks and in *italics* (where appropriate), for example "quilombo" (or *quilombo*) and *kilombo*; "Umbanda" and *umbanda*. In addition, the African italicized concepts are written in lowercase.

Some African-Brazilian concepts, like Samba, Candomblé and Umbanda are in the meantime also widely recognized in other languages. In these cases the quotation marks have been omitted. Finally we note that this differentiation does not apply for direct quotations from literature since source-critical considerations may not be altered.

Regarding the presentation and comparability of African terms: we have here the issue that there is just as much a deficiency of a consistent orthographic system for these as there is for European words. There are different orthographies for Africa's many languages and it is not uncommon for them to be based on phonological aspects.[1] In some West African languages, for example Ewe and Fon, phonetic symbols have been introduced (by Dietrich Westermann). In contract to this, the Yorùbá language today still utilizes anarchic orthography introduced by nineteenth-century missionaries. It contains numerous diacritical marks: e for phon. [ɛ], o for phon. [ɔ] and ṣ as in the word Ṣangó (Brazilian: "Xangô"), wherein the [ʃ] is to be spoken with pursed lips.

We cannot change the existing orthographic systems, even

i

though they occasionally complicate our cross-language comparison of related or identical words.

In deviation from one of the common customs of older Bantu studies—omitting the prefixes from certain nominatives when writing cultural or "ethnic" names—we have decided not to do so. However, we do often retain the plural prefixes, for example, Valuchazi (plural term) or Luchazi, a people in East Angola; their language is Luchazi (with no prefix).

FOREWORD

Major portions of this text were written in mid-1981, one year following my return from my fourth research- and presentation trip to Brazil. It is based on field work from 1974, 1975, 1979, and, most recently, 1980. This final segment was done in collaboration with two African associates, Moya Aliya Malamusi and Donald Kachamba from Malawi, as well as the Brazilian folklore scholar Guilherme dos Santos Barbosa from São Paulo. My data collection in Brazil was based on previous field work I'd done in many years on the African continent, whereby the most relevant stays were in Angola (1965, 1979, 1981 and 1982); in Nigeria and Dahomey (1960), in Nigeria (1963, 1973 and 1974) and in Togo (1970).

A pre-publication of text sections of this book appeared in 1981 and 1982 in the *Wiener Ethnohistorische Blätter* (nos. 21 and 22) published by the Ethnological Institute at the University of Vienna. The numerous elements of positive feedback and valuable supplementary material I received from many, many colleagues following that first publication have, to a large extent, been integrated into this book. Similarly, the approx. 35 participants of the seminar on cultural investigation which I held in Luanda in 1982 (18 January – 2 March) at the invitation of the Departamento Nacional de Folclore (Director: Virgilio R.C. Coelho) have likewise contributed valuable informational material. They also held discussions with me about my Brazilian material as observed from an Angolan point of view.

I would like to extend my thanks to the associates mentioned above as well as to numerous Brazilian colleagues, in particular Tiago de Oliveira Pinto, for the many hours of discussion in Berlin, Vienna and Lisboa, and for the review of the final manuscript. I would also like to express my gratitude to the Goethe Institutes in Brazil and the headquarters in Munich; the Centro de Estudos Africanos at the University of São Paulo (Director: Fernando A. Mourão); and the Departamento de Ciências Sociais at that university (Director: João Baptista Borges Pereira) for their invitations in various contexts to come to Brazil. Finally, I extend my thanks to the Fonds zur Förderung der Wissenschaftlichen Forschung (FWF, the Austrian Science Fund), Vienna, for financing our 1980 field research in Brazil (project no. 4210).

Gerhard Kubik

INTRODUCTION

African cultures were transplanted to Brazil through transatlantic slaving from the sixteenth to the nineteenth centuries. They still exist there today in mutated and mixed forms amongst populations of predominantly African descent. These African cultures have also had a notable influence on European-Brazilian segments of the population. According to the most recent 2010 census, approximately 51 percent of Brazil's population of 191 million demonstrate distinct characteristics pointing to African origin. The cultural heritage of Africa is particularly evident in the areas of music and dance, verbal culture ("oral literature"), religious beliefs, Bahia's cuisine, children's games, arts and crafts techniques and many other areas; in the distinct African language remnants still found in many regions; and finally, in the Brazilian philosophy on life.

Seen from a historical perspective, the migration of African population elements to the Americas presents quite a multi-facetted picture. It was a process encompassing many aspects, and the emphasis on any particular aspect was continuously fluid over the course of three and a half centuries. From the nineteenth century onwards the population flow to Brazil saw a parallel population and cultural flow back into African areas, above all to the West African coast. A concentrated cultural exchange along the lines of a transatlantic triangle (Brazil – Nigeria – Angola) began early on.

There is a long history of investigation into the cultural relationships between Brazil and Africa. Recently, extensive reorientation in terms of research concepts, perspectives and methods, as well as the engagement of African researchers (both indigenous as well as non-indigenous people working there), has stimulated investigation in a variety of new ways. In African diaspora studies during the 1940s—a period synonymous with the name of eminent anthropologist Melville J. Herskovits—cultural research concerning the African diaspora was basically a research into acculturation. One of its main objectives was to research how and by what processes Africans adapted to western cultures in the Americas.²

The Cuban cultural scholar Fernando Ortiz had already expressed his reservations of accepting the acculturation concept as a universal model. He suggested instead the concept of "transculturation," emphasizing the reciprocity inherent in a cultural exchange to describe many of the processes and outcomes in the African diaspora area. The main contradictions in the methods employed in African diaspora studies in the forties were grounded in the different treatment of people of African descent living in America as compared to indigenous Africans on their home soil.

While African diasporic cultures in the Americas were often analyzed from a *historical* perspective (i.e., following the historical method: evaluation of written, iconographic and verbal sources), scholars of cultures on the African continent – of which the African diaspora were a continuation – contented themselves with an *ahistorical* approach. Caught up in the stereotype of the "continent without a history," scholars attempted to interpret the African portion of African diasporic history with the help of the "roots" concept but with total disregard for principals of continuity. This incongruous view of the African diasporic and African scenes, often presented by the same author, led to contradictions in methodology. The idea of looking for "roots" of an existent culture is like a concept of cultural morphology best described as a "tree model." In such a model, a culture can be represented in a pseudo-historical context by the form of a tree. Thinking in terms of an overall history comprising Africa and Afro-America, one could scientifically examine the "branches" and the "leafy sections" according to historical methods. On the other hand, one would take an ahistorical approach with the "roots," looking through the lens of an evolutionary framework and believing that African cultures are "traditional" and haven't changed much over the course of centuries or even millennia.

The history of the African diaspora is essentially regarded as a history of acculturation, that is, not as his "own" history (which he's not regarded as capable of having). It's the history of his adaptation to Old World culture. From this point of view, the history of the African diaspora began in the moment he stepped onto American soil. Whatever happened before that was, at best, "prehistory" or "roots."

It is no longer possible today to work in this framework in African diaspora studies, and certainly not in African studies. One cannot attribute African diaspora cultural phenomena to "roots" somewhere in Africa and be over and done with it. Rather, wherever one goes to seek historical connections with Africa, it is essential to approach material *on both sides* of the Atlantic with identical investigative methods and observe the principles of synchrony and diachronic in the sense of historical method. Even if I can prove that certain Yorùbá elements exist in "Candomblé" religious practices around Bahia, this is by far not the end of the discussion. The next questions are: Which Yorùbá cultural elements are they? Which epochs of Yorùbá culture in Nigeria and along the Dahomey coast do they represent? From exactly which cultural-geographic areas within Yorùbá-speaking territory do they come? Within the current-day Yorùbá cultural area there are significant differences between the Ọ̀yọ̀-, Ondo-, Ijesha-, Ekiti- and other Yorùbá subgroups; and apart from this, all these Yorùbá subcultures were somewhat different in the seventeenth, eighteenth and nineteenth centuries from what they are today.

In principle it must be noted that the transplantation of very disparate African cultural complexes and elements over the course of more than three centuries in the Americas was a selective process. That is to be expected. Staying with the Yorùbá example, it was not the full breadth of the Yorùbá cultural panorama that was transplanted to the Americas, but rather those aspects of certain cultures corresponding to indigenous areas of the deported people and the degree to which each of these individuals asserted themselves vis-à-vis the others.

A jostling for position amongst the Africans themselves started within the various groups thrown together right after their recruitment into slavery. There began a cultural selection which continued on the soil of the Americas. Those individuals with "soft voices" were simply silenced, in a cultural sense, by the majority. Thus an African-internal selection process began on American soil before cultural contact with the Old World could even take hold. This may not be confused with Melville J. Herskovits's concept of selection, which, in its practical application, referred almost exclusively to acculturation processes triggered through contact of the Africans with the European cultural world.

In any case, one has to imagine African and African diaspora regional cultures along a timeline on both continents running parallel and synchronous to each other. The opportunities opened up by transatlantic ship traffic, which facilitated a constant reciprocal influence between specific African cultural zones and neo-African cultural zones springing up from them in the Americas were also significant. The Atlantic Ocean was not as much of a cultural barrier as one might imagine. The bridge back to Africa was in no way burned for deported people after their arrival in the Americas. News from the homeland trickled in one way or another, and that from America also reached the African continent. There are countless oral traditions that recall these contacts on both sides of the Atlantic, and occasionally there is tangible evidence on African soil pointing to this alternating flow of ideas and cultural stuff (e.g. "Brazilian architecture" in Lagos, Ibadan, Oshogbo and other Yorùbá cities in West Nigeria). There are also collections like the private one of Hubert Kponton in Lomé, Togo, or those in government museums like the Museu de Escravatura in Angola or the Slave House on the Ile de Gorée near Dakar, Senegal, where this constant *flux* and *reflux* is also impressively documented (cf. Verger 1968).

AFRICAN POPULATIONS IN BRAZIL: CULTURAL GROUP CONSTITUTION AND ORIGINS

Historians' opinions differ about the date that the first Africans stepped onto Brazilian soil. Some believe that two or more Africans were on board the ships of Pedro Alvares Cabral when he accidently landed on the Brazilian coast on 24 April 1500. Portuguese settlers began systematic colonization around 1530. It seems that 1538 was the year in which the first shipment of enslaved Africans, bound for the sugar cane plantations, was brought to Brazil. As the sugar cane industry intensified, and, later, diamonds, silver and gold were discovered in eastern Brazil, the need for slave labor became insatiable. In 1583 the Jesuit missionary José de Anchieta wrote that around 14,000 Africans were in Brazil—10,000 in Pernambuco, 3,000 in Bahia and 1,000 in Rio de Janeiro (Cassiano 1940; Porter 1978, xiii).

At the beginning of the nineteenth century Africans constituted the majority of the population of Rio de Janeiro.[3] The city's street-life and the lifestyle of its inhabitants most likely bore a resemblance to Luanda. Up until the middle of the nineteenth century, the highest concentrations of the population with economic and cultural significance were located in the country's east and northeast: in Bahia and Pernambuco, and in particular the rain-blessed coastal zone. The dry *sertão* in the country's interior, on the other hand, was an impoverished region, as is the case today.

Johann Moritz Rugendas noted the breakdown of Brazil's total population of around 4 million in 1835 as follows: 1,987,500 enslaved Africans; 159,500 formerly enslaved individuals; 416,000 "coloreds" and 843,000 whites (Rugendas 1835, 20). These proportions shifted notably in the second half of the nineteenth and the first half of the twentieth centuries, when major immigration from Europe—mostly from Italy, Spain and Portugal—took place as a result of the Industrial Revolution.

In particular, immigrants settled in the southern part of the country and contributed to the population explosion and industrialization of South America's henceforth largest city, São Paulo. The population profile of Rio de Janeiro, Brazil's capital city from 1763 to 1960, also changed quickly. People of African descent were pushed increasingly from the low-elevation city districts to the *favelas* (slums) and the *morros* (granite mountains). The majority of this urban-fringe population today comprises migrants from the northeast (Bahia, Sergipe, Alagoas and Pernambuco), who have been flooding into the metropolises in recent decades.

From which parts of Africa did the ancestors of today's African-Brazilian population segments come? At risk of oversimplification, we can divide these areas into two large regions:

1. The region of south-western Nigeria including Dahomey (also called "Benin," in French pronunciation) and adjoining areas. These Africans who were abducted to Brazil were mostly various subgroups of the Yorùbá people in Brazil collectively called Nagô, Fon and Ewe ("Gêge" in the Brazilian language); Igbo from the eastern side of the Niger delta, and Nupe from the Niger-Benue hinterland.

2. The so-called Angola/Congo area, which comprises almost all of Angola, south-western Congo, Cabinda, parts of Congo-Brazzaville and regions stretching far into the interior of Central Africa, like the Lunda/Luvale region in the confluence zone of Angola, Zambia and Congo (Katanga).

Besides these large cultural regions, some of the origin of enslaved Africans in Brazil can be ascribed, to a smaller extent, to Southeast Africa. These people were transported to Brazil from the regions of Inhambane and the Zambezi Valley in Mozambique (Quelimane), as well as from the Nyasa/Ruvuma region in northern Mozambique and Malawi. An interesting case study of transatlantic slaving in Mozambique can be found in the published work of António Carreira (1979).

An additional zone was the savanna hinterland of the entire stretch of West African coastline from Senegal and Guinea-Bissau to Nigeria. There the number of people who had been brought to Brazil was relatively small; mainly they were Hausa and Manding, as well as some several smaller ethnicities. Some of these Sudanese minorities pursued a career in Brazil as illusionists, "magicians" and snake charmers. This was the origin of the expression "mandingueiros" (fr. Manding), meaning magician. In his chapter "Customs and Practices of the Negroes," Rugendas reports on the peripheral position of this group in the cultural fabric of Rio de Janeiro during the first half of the nineteenth century:

> Something that is especially feared is the effect of the so-called *mandingua*, a sort of talisman, with which the *mandingueiro* slowly kills either those who have done him wrong or others he wants to hurt or can "give it to them" in any other way. The *mandingua* is made of a large mass of herbs, roots, soil and animal-ingredients which are bound together while reciting all kinds of magic spells. Then it is placed either in or under the bed of the person being targeted.... Although *mandingos* are hated and feared, and not revered, by the Negroes, and although many Negroes reject belief in these things as ungodly, these people still have a notable influence on their environment. They are occasionally the cause of serious disorders and crimes to such an extent that in one district peace and order can often be restored only by removal of a *mandingo* (Rugendas 1835, 29).

The zone exhibiting the strongest presence of an African population in Brazil today lies within an approximately 500 kilometer-wide swath of land comprising all of eastern Brazil. This area starts at Pernambuco and runs along the curve of the lower Rio São Francisco to Rio de Janeiro, with tendrils stretching into the area of Sorocaba south of São Paulo. In addition, there are several predominant African population islands in the interior of Brazil, like Vila Bela da Santíssima Trindade, the former capital of Mato Grosso, as well as some spots in the north (in Maranhão, Pará, etc.).

The life of the enslaved, particularly in rural areas, was highly structured in all the details of daily life. Johann Moritz Rugendas

(1835), one of our most valuable sources from the early nineteenth century, describes the living conditions of the enslaved on the plantations (*roças*) as follows:

> During the sugar cane harvest, for example, work continues day and night, with crews of Negroes relieving each other like sailors on a ship. The harvest lasts from the end of September until the end of October, and during this time everything is done to keep the Negroes hale and hearty—so it is loud and jolly to start. Only gradually do the slaves become exhausted from the relentless work, particularly in the sugar mills (*engenhos*), so that, regardless where they find themselves, they fall asleep from fatigue. This is where the saying comes from: *he dorminhoço como negro de engenho* (he is as sleepy as a Negro in a sugar mill). Quite often weariness leads to accidents while a Negro is feeding sugar cane into the rollers. Perhaps his hand or a bit of his clothing gets caught; and occasionally the whole arm and sometimes the whole body is squashed if there's no one there immediately to help. On some plantations there is a strong iron pole next to the machine which, when this happens, is thrust between the rollers to stop them or force them apart. Often, however, the victim can only be saved by immediately taking a hatchet and hacking off the finger, the hand or the arm that was caught in the rollers (Rugendas 1835, 9-10).

African-Brazilians were still classified according to *nação* (nations) up to about the end of the nineteenth century. Some of the recognized groups were the Nagô, Gêge, Mandingo, Mina, Angola, Congo, Benguela, Rebolo, Mozambique, etc.[4] Only a few of these names are based on African ethnicities; their function was to serve as brand names with which abducted people could be assigned to larger overarching groups in both ethnic and regional senses. A Brazilian customer associated certain qualities and character traits of the "product" with these trade names. These characteristics are described over and over again in the documentation of the period.

Thus the expression "Nagô" refers not only to Yorùbá people from Dahomey, but also includes groups on the outer edge of the Yorùbá dialect area in Nigeria. "Benguela" refers to the Bay of Benguela in Angola, where large numbers of people, many of them from the distant interior of Angola, were sold by Ovimbundu slave traders to the Portuguese. They usually had some knowledge of the local language, Umbundu, but belonged to completely different ethnic groups, for example Nkhumbi, Handa, Cilenge and others from the province known today as Wila ("Huíla") as well as various Ngangela-speaking groups from the regions of East Angola. "Angola" referred to the area of the former Kingdom of Ndongo (under Ngola rulers) where Kimbundu was spoken. The inhabitants called themselves Imbundu or Akwakimbundu (sing. Kimbundu or Mukwakimbundu). "Congo" often refers to a greater extent to the former vassal states of the old Kingdom of Kôngo rather than the main one, and includes a wide variety of ethnic groups in North Angola and in southwest Congo (now Democratic Republic of Congo) through to Congo-Brazzaville.

In 1816, Henry Koster states that the enslaved Africans brought to Pernambuco during his time were known by the following names: "Angola," "Congo," "Rebolo," "Anjico," "Gabão" and "Mozambique."[5] He then describes the "character" of each individual nation, praising the docile traits of the "Angola" group followed by the "Congo" and "Rebolo" groups. He writes that the importatation of Gabonese to Brazil had started only recently, and that they were rumoured to be "man-eaters" and showed a high incidence of suicide.[6] Their selling price was low compared to captives from "Angola." The very lowest price was that for the "Mozambiques"; they were "weak" and "lazy," and tended to depression. Pernambuco never experienced serious revolts from the enslaved such as those in Bahia, although many more formerly enslaved Africans lived there. This was due, according to Koster, to the fact that very few came from the "Gold Coast" (by which he meant the entire Guinea Coast and Nigeria); in Bahia, the majority of the population came from there. The view that the Yorùbá-speaking West Africans in Brazil, who in Henry Koster's time were concentrated in Bahia, were more inclined to revolt and aggression than the Angola/Congo group in the south and in Pernambuco is shared by numerous authors, including Rugendas.

Rugendas (1835) drew many portraits of Africans in Brazil, whom he identified by "nations." In the chapter "Portraits and Costumes" he writes that Brazil, specifically Rio de Janeiro, is perhaps the only, and in any case the most favorable, place on earth

> where such a wide selection of the typical physiognomies of various Negro groups is found; because the unusual lot of this race has brought members of Negro groups from almost all corners of Africa to one market. This gives the artist the opportunity to achieve something that even in Africa itself would only be hard-won fruit after long and dangerous travels through all parts of the region. One cannot even find a place in America offering this ease of access, since at this moment Brazil enjoys the infamous reputation of being the only country where slave trade is actually carried out without any limitations whatsoever....
>
> The Negro cultural groups to which most of the slaves brought into Brazil belong are the Angolas, Benguelas, Manjolos, Congos, Rebolos, Anjicos and Minas from the African west coast, and the Mozambiques from the east coast. As shown in the drawings of Negro heads, they can be differentiated from one another partly by the special facial tattoos and partly by very marked differences in the physiognomy. Some groups display very little of the characteristic features usually noted of the African race. They do, however, differentiate themselves by certain variations in temperament and character which has resulted in a better or worst reputation, depending on the tribe, in the general public opinion. The Mina and Angola Negroes, for example, are said to make the best slaves. They are gentle, docile and it is easy to win their loyal devotion if they are treated well. At the same time, however, these are also the ones most

likely to be in a position to buy their freedom because they work hard and are frugal. The Congos are in many ways like the Angolas, but they are clumsy and more accustomed to rough field work. The Rebolos likewise can hardly be differentiated from these two; the languages of these three groups are also quite similar. However, the Rebolos are more headstrong and inclined to melancholy than the other two.

The Anjicos are larger and better proportioned, and have fewer of the African facial features than the aforementioned five. They are bolder and wily, and have a greater love of freedom. They should be treated especially well so as to avoid losing them due to an escape, or experiencing confrontation from them. The Minas can be identified by three hemispherical scars that stretch from the corner of the mouth to the ear. The Gabanis are wilder and more unruly than all the previous ones. Their mortality rate is the highest because they have the most difficulty adapting to the work and the slavery. They are also large and muscular. Their skin is a glistening black, their facial features exhibit minimal African traits. The Monjolos are the least prized; they are often small, weak and ugly, lazy and dispirited. Their color is somewhat brownish; and they fetch the worst price (Rugendas 1835, 11, 29).

Historical studies of transatlantic slaving in Brazil, particularly regarding the areas of origin for the enslaved, are often difficult, since a large part of the archival documents in Rio de Janeiro were burned in an 1891 *autodafé* by abolitionists after the 1888 abolition. However, even documents which have been preserved can often be a source of serious errors. Fernando A. A. Mourão, Director of the Centro de Estudos Africanos at the University of São Paulo, points to the following example of São Tomé:

As to the question of actual origins, the errors are systematic. It is common among the majority of authors to make reference to slaves from São Tomé, while in fact São Tomé was only a place of passage. This island was only inhabited during the era of the navigations, and the people working there came from the continent. Such errors are so widespread that it seems unnecessary to cite other examples. And yet one speaks generically of the Bantu as geographically cohesive which also does not correspond to reality. We believe that it is necessary to proceed from a revision of the framework that refers to the origins of the slaves, rather than limiting ourselves to the schema adopted by authors such as Nina Rodrigues and Arthur Ramos, thereby giving the impression that the subject has been treated sufficiently.[7]

Relatively detailed data on the origin of former enslaved Africans is available from the Bahia region, thanks to research by Pierre Verger (1968). This is the area of Brazil where the African population elements and cultural heritage is so predominant that a lucrative business of folklore tourism has mushroomed. It is here that refined neo-African cultural expressions developed. In most quarters of the city Salvador/Bahia, in particular, one encounters the culture of the African communities from the region of the Golf of Benin (southwest Nigeria and Dahomey). There are the famous manifestations of African-Brazilian religions, Yorùbá religious practices concerning the orişa (written here as "orixá" regularly announced in newspapers like *Viver Bahia*), and open to the general public. But West African culture is also visible in all areas of life—from music and dance to the famous Bahian cuisine. Even with only a fleeting familiarity with some Yorùbá terms, like *akara* (little balls made of beans and fried in oil; here, *acarajé*), one can easily make one's way through the city without having to speak Portuguese.

Pierre Verger's work is based upon studies kept in the Arquivo Público da Bahia; the Arquivo Histórico Ultramarino, Lisboa; the Archives Nationales de Paris; and in the Public Records Office, London. He concluded that transatlantic slaving epoch can be divided into three historical periods spanning various areas of Africa:

1. From about 1550 to 1600 enslaved Africans came predom-

inantly from West Africa via harbors on the Guinea coast to Bahia.

2. From about 1600 to 1700 the majority of those abducted came from the Congo/Angola area.

3. From 1700 to 1770 slave trade shifted back to West Africa. Most of the enslaved Africans came from the "Mina Coast."

In the final phase, from 1770 to 1850, most came from southwest Nigeria and Dahomey and were members of the Nagô/Yorùbá group.

Verger raises a yellow flag about many citations in the sources and recommends that one approach their interpretation with caution. For example, "Mina" does not necessarily mean a person from Ghana (i.e., the area around the Elmina). He says,

> In Brazil those who were called Mina blacks were not enslaved Africans who came from the Gold Coast, but they had been obtained through any of the four ports already mentioned: Grand Popo, Ouidah, Jaquin and Apa.
>
> We will see how, from the second third of the seventeenth century, the slave trade was shifting to the east of Ouidah, to new ports called Porto Novo, Badagry and Lagos (then named Onim), thereby giving rise to [what we have called] the cycle of the Gulf of Benin. There the slave trade continued clandestinely with tenacious intensity until 1851, in spite of the treaties signed by Great Britain, Portugal and Brazil to abolish the trade north of the equator from 1815 onward.[8]

Verger argues that the prevalence of Yorùbá customs and traditions in Bahia may be explained by the arrival of countless Yorùbá peoples and related West African groups during the last slave trade period, part of which was already an underground activity. The theory that the most recent arrivals of African populations and cultural elements in Brazil made the strongest and longest-lasting impact is attributed to Verger.

Following the 1815 treaty between the Atlantic maritime

powers forbidding slave trade north of the equator, transatlantic slaving intensified on the routes between the harbors of Angola and Mozambique to Rio de Janeiro and, to a certain extent, to Pernambuco. As a result, the situation in the south was much different than that in Bahia. Through the last phase of transatlantic slaving the majority of people brought to Rio de Janeiro and São Paulo were from Bantu regions of Africa, above all from the Congo/Angola area.[9]

As early as the eighteenth century a new phase began in Brazil, one which I would call a "secondary proliferation" of African population elements and cultures. Up until around 1700 Brazil was the world's largest producer of sugar. This epoch of Brazilian history is therefore often called the *ciclo do açúcar* (sugar cycle). Following the discovery of gold and diamonds in Minas Gerais, economic activity shifted slightly from monocultural plantations to mining. This period is known as the *ciclo do ouro* (gold cycle). Enslaved Africans were sold into those other parts of Brazil which were designated for economic development, in particular Minas Gerais. Later, voluntary laborer immigration took place on a large scale. Thus Bahia was infiltrated in the late nineteenth century by Africans of mostly Angolan origin coming from southern Brazil. They brought along their autonomous cultures from the western Bantu-speaking part of Central Africa. Many elements of clearly Angolan origins have survived to the present day in the classic sugar cane region, the Recôncavo Baiano. The development of the large industrial centers in the south of the country, precipitated by concentrated European (above all, Italian) immigration during the first decades of the twentieth century, brought a change in migrant orientation within Brazil, with many Bahians moving to the south as laborers.

One of the most important sources enabling (almost unintentionally) an historical division of transatlantic slaving according to African ethnicity and region of origin is the 1848 investigation by the missionary and linguist Sigismund W. Koelle into the languages of formerly enslaved Africans in Freetown, Sierra Leone. Looking for a comparable vocabulary for the largest possible number of African languages spoken on various parts of the continent, he asked formerly enslave Africans brought ashore by the British Marines in Sierra Leone about their mother tongue.[10]

Philip Curtin extrapolated Koelle's data from this representative segment of enslaved Africans to create a cartographical model showing area of origin.[11]

Koelle's linguistic survey shows, for example, amongst those abducted from the Nigeria-Dahomey-Togo region, pockets of concentration as follows: Dahomey/Togo: Ese, Adja, Hueda or Aizo, Fon, Mahi; Nigeria: a) Yorùbá subgroups such as Egbado, Egba, Ijesha, Oyo, Yagba, Ekiti, Jumu, Aworo, Ijebu, Ife, Ondo, Itsekiri, Igala. Of these there were particularly large numbers of Oyo (several thousand individuals). Yorùbá speakers comprised by far the largest number of freed enslaved Africans; b) members of the Niger-Benue language group such as Nupe, Jupa, Dibo, Gbari, Kakanda or Basange, Ebe, Igbira-Panda, Igbira-Hima; and c) members of the Niger Delta language group: Igbo (with subgroups Isu-Ama, Ishielu, Abaja, Aro, Mbofia), Urhobo, Etsako, Benin, Ishan, Olomo, Ijaw.

Even for the Congo/Angola area, for which the British military freed a much smaller number of enslaved Africans since the slave ships usually took routes south of the Equator, there are these valuable details: Cabinda/Congo/Zaïre: Vili, Mboma, Ntandu, Kaniok, Teke, Tsaye, Tio, Mbeti, Yombe, Nsundi, Lunda; and Angola: Imbangala, Ambundu, Ovimbundu, Lweda, Songo, and Sama.

For Southeast Africa (Mozambique and Malawi), the following Koelle data are available: Yao, Cuabo, Maravi, Makwa, South Makwa, and Inhambane. The fact that each individual's year of imprisonment as well as the number of individuals in each group at Sierra Leone were also recorded is particularly valuable for those examining the data. It suffices for our purposes to cite the "modern" names of the ethnic groups as we have done above. However, it should be noted that Koelle's original nomenclature deviates from Curtin's "translation" and that the latter is not without its problems. Koelle's original designations (noted as spoken word from his subjects) of the six above groups from Angola were: Kasands or Kasandsi, Ngola, Benguela or Pangela, Lubalo or Balubalo, Songo, and Kisama.

All these names need to be interpreted carefully. For example, equating "Benguela" or "Pangela" with "Ovimbundu" is erroneous because the latter rarely sold those of their own group.

Groups from the hinterland of the Bay of Benguela were classified as "Benguela" who knew the Umbundu common language (of the Ovimbundu slave traders) fairly well, but came from completely different ethnic groups. "Ngola," mentioned as being particularly numerous, are a Kimbundu-speaking group from the hinterland of Luanda. "Lubalo" or "Balubalo" refers to the Luvale (plural prefix, Valuvale). The Mozambique segment is also more revealing in the original version: Koelle wrote "Kiriman" instead of Cuabo, referring to the coastal town of Quelimane. Makwa is replaced by "Meto," a Makua subgroup concentrated in Northern Mozambique with which I am quite familiar.

Transatlantic slaving extended deep into inner Africa, particularly during the nineteenth century, as evidenced in Koelle's and many others' written and oral sources. Trade middlemen associated with particular ethnic groups specialized in human trafficking in the various regions. They made verbal agreements with local village chiefs and often financed armed attacks on villages. One such middle-man ethnic group was the indigenous Ovimbundu living in the Viye (Bié) highlands in Central Angola. They developed a multi-branched trade route whose main artery ran along today's Benguela railway (which still follows this old trade route) and continued into the region of the old Lunda Kingdom. The trade goods included ivory, captive Africans, rubber, wax and many other products that were brought to the Atlantic coast where they were purchased by Portuguese buyers.

Others involved in slave trading were Arabs from the east, Swahili, Yao (in the Ruvuma/Nyasa region, and in northeastern Zambia), and Bisa. In the middle of the nineteenth century the eastern and western slave trade met at several points in Central Africa. At that time the Angola trade stretched deep into Katanga. Analysis of oral traditions from these areas serves us well in illuminating unexplained questions. The Luvale historian Mose Kaputungu Sangambo (b. 1902), well-travelled in parts of Angola, Zambia and Congo in his search for his ancestors' history, described the mechanism of transatlantic slaving in Central Africa:

> Slavery did not start as a result of trade with the Ovimbundu but slavery increased because of the trade. It was the custom in the ancient days to make defeat-

ed enemies slaves.... But these slaves were a part of the village. A man could be judged by the number of slaves he had, just as today men are judged by the wealth and number of servants they have....

There were many ways of enslaving people other than war. Sometimes someone borrowed something and failed to repay it; that person could become a slave to pay off the debt. Even a relative of someone who owed a debt could be given as a slave....

Then there is also *Tukaza*, a magic crocodile that catches people when they are fishing, especially beautiful women. We find a special medicine, an image of the person, left by the pond but the person is gone. Another way is called *oholi* where a person appears to die and is 'buried,' but actually something else was buried while the person was taken and sold. Even chiefs were using these medicines to enslave people.

The Ovimbundu paid for slaves with cloth, guns, blankets, gunpowder, beads, knives, salt and many other things. It is said that one gun or two or three *tupesa* of cloth (one *kapesa* equals about eight yards) would buy one slave. Sometimes even more was paid.

The slaves which brought the greatest prices were young women who could bear children. Next were full grown men, and after that children. But the most important was the young woman.

The Ovimbundu were not the only ones who came for slaves. Even the Portuguese came and then there were the Swahili. Chief Chiwala at Ndola is the descendant of chiefs who came for slaves. Near Kavungu in Angola there are Sachiwiwi and Kabombola who came originally as slave traders. Today they have even married my relatives and have children with them. We have even been told about the Yeke people who came from the Congo for slaves and who fought Chief Mshili's people.

But the main people looking for slaves were the Ovimbundu. They used to bring salt to trade. If someone said the Ovimbundu had come he was asked to show the salt to prove their arrival.

The Ovimbundu did not catch slaves themselves. They only bought slaves from their owners. As more and more Ovimbundu came into our country they wanted more and more slaves. It was a time when no person was safe.

This was a terrible time for the people. The Ovimbundu wanted too many slaves and some chiefs even sold their own people for guns. People were afraid to travel and had to live in large, stockaded villages in order to protect themselves....

The Ovimbundu transported the slaves in caravans. They used a wooden yoke made from a tree with a fork at both ends so that two slaves were bound around the neck. At night sometimes the legs of the slaves were tied. The slaves were treated very badly, not like slaves in the villages.

I remember when the Europeans stopped transatlantic slaving and outlawed slavery. Many slaves were freed. This was called *kulukulula*—a Lozi word meaning to 'give up.' I saw this with my own eyes. Some owners were very reluctant to give up their slaves. Many complaints were made to the Europeans and some owners were arrested for refusing to free their slaves (Sangambo 1979, 76-78).

The African perspective is undeniably present in this report of actual events, partly related by eyewitnesses during the last phase of transatlantic slaving in the Land of the Luvale along the border of Angola, Zambia and Congo. This phase lasted into the twentieth century. There are a large number of unexamined sources regarding transatlantic slaving, both in the African oral traditions and in records kept by Africans. In addition, numerous objects from the slavery era still exist and are often in the possession of families whose ancestors had a connection to slave traders, or who had slave traders in their families or households. One example is the collection of artefacts which the Togolese Hubert Kponton (1905-1981) kept in his private museum in Rue Kuassibruce, Lomé, Togo. Kponton relates the following about his own past and these objects:

> My deceased mother Adjoavidjé Apollonia Kponton is a descendant of one of the abandoned children of the Brazilian slave trader Félix Francisco de Souza, who bought the Peninsula of Adjido (Anecho) around 1789 from King Sekpon, the only son of Quam-Dessou. King Gezo of Dahomé was a good friend of this slave trader.[12]

The objects from the historical slavery period had been family possessions for a long time, and included, amongst others, a Danish firearm of the type that the slave traders (*négriers*) used to give the king of Porto Seguro to beat back revolts; a plate from Salvador/Bahia belonging to Francisco O. Silva from Porto Seguro; and iron chains, neck shackles and arm-cuffs used to fetter enslaved Africans together and prevent them from escaping. Also amongst the collection was a metal gag (*bâillon*) to keep the enslaved Africans from crying out, as well as a board to hold their hands together, and a hinged neck chain (*collier à charnière*).

Kponton also mentioned the crops which the Brazilian slave traders introduced to his hometown (Anecho in Togo): manioc, including the technology of tapioca production; corn; mangos; and certain types of bananas and cocoa—this last item arriving via the island of São Tomé. Only the "wild banana" (*la banana sauvage*) was known here before the arrival of the Europeans.[13]

Oral testimonies also indicate that slave trading was viewed unfavorably by those affected. There are *noŋano*, stories and fairy tales of the Ovahanda people, whose province Wila ("Huíla") in southwest Angola was literally depopulated by transatlantic slaving flow to the Bay of Benguela. Even today, this issue is anchored in the historical conscience of the locals and is expressed in the narratives that are part of every young person's upbringing. These stories have been accorded their own category in the Luhanda language, that of *noŋano vyovapika* (stories of the enslaved). Even though the plots are fictional, like stories, they depict memories derived from actual happenings during the time of slavery in southwest Angola.

The Angolan cultural scholar Marcelina Gomes, who participated in my seminar "Introdução à metodologia das pesquisas culturais" at the Departamento Nacional de Folclore, Luanda (1 January 1982 – 2 March 1982) cited several examples after returning from the two-week practical field research. *Twende kumukwata* (Let's go! Catch him/her!) and *kumukuta* (bind him/her), among others, are frequent images in such stories, and they have lost none of their emotional impact even today. There is always a song in the *noŋano* stories which is sung by all participants at a storytelling and which highlights particularly dramatic points in the plot. *Ovapika* (sing. *omupika*) is the term for "slaves" in Luhanda. Since slavery in this region, as in east Angola (cf. Sangambo, above), was an historical institution practiced in the framework of traditional law, these stories were not just about transatlantic slaving in the Americas. The Ovahanda have several sub-types of slave stories. As described in one of the stories told by Marcelina Gomes about a slave who in the end became a free son (*munaŋana*) of a chief, an *Omupika* house slave could gain his freedom under certain conditions.[14]

In order to escape slavery themselves, many traditional chiefs and their subjects entered partnerships with ethnicities whose people were allied with Portuguese and other slave traders on the coasts of West and Central Africa, and who themselves were engaged in transatlantic slaving. A classic case in Angola was the Ovimbundu (language: Umbundu). In the nineteenth century, in particular, the Ovimbundu were a significant economic body thanks to their trading of enslaved Africans, salt, wax and ivory with the people of East Angola, whom they called Vangangeìa (People of the Dawn). The cultural influence, originating in Central Angola, of the Ovimbundu—intermediaries between the Portuguese living on the coast and the inland peoples—expanded far beyond their own borders. Their language, Umbundu, became the most important tongue in Angola. In the eastern part of the country, the Valucazi people (who originally, as the ethnic name implies, had settled at the Lucazi River southeast of the city of Vila Luso (present-day Lwena), near the present Benguela rail line) still remember those times. The Lucazi historian Luka Katyapa Kangamba wrote as follows:

> Vakele nakuya kuchikumo chaKalunga kukeko vakele nakulandesa zimbinga zyavanjamba, sela, kenya, kwiza hakatikati, vakele nakulandesa navandungo, vaLuchazi kavakele muvundungo kumiyati yaveka chahi, vakevo vakele nakwenda, kwose muNjenje, muLunda, muVulamba, muMbwela, nakulengeya vupite nakumona mafuti. Vendele nakuheta kukalungandonga (Atlantic Ocean) oku namuno muLyambezi, vakele nakuheta muKasavi, naLwalava, nakulengeya vupite ... mata avo vakele nakusekasyana nasela, nakenya navandungo, kaha kuvindele kwafumine mata nazimpota, natutalelo, navimbilingwa, namaseka, namintsele, navyuma vyavingi vyavundele. Vimbundu vakele masamba vavo muvakele vakusekasyanena...
>
> (They went to the coast of the sea, where they sold elephant teeth, wax and rubber. On the way they also sold slaves. The Valuchazi were not slaves of other groups; rather, they travelled all over into the regions of Njenje, Lunda, Vulamba and Mbwela looking for trading goods and to see other countries. On their journeys they came to the sea (the Atlantic Ocean) and from there then back to the Zambezi. They came to the Kasavi people and the Lwalava people who were looking for goods to trade.... They got their weapons in trade for wax, rubber and slaves. The Europeans traded firearms, glass pearls, mirrors, earrings, bracelets made of wire and hair, and bracelets made of metal and many things of European origin. The Ovimbundu were their friends, and they enjoyed an economic relationship....)[15]

The "Museu da Escravatura" (Museum of Slavery) in Morro da Cruz, 23 kilometers from Luanda, Angola. Numerous historical artefacts from the time of slavery are preserved here.

The renovated building in which the Museum of the MPLA Government of Angola is housed (Arch. no. B 661)

Chains and locks used to fetter abducted enslaved Africans together (B 667)

A so-called "bola de escravo" (slave ball), weighing around 15 kilograms, attached to the legs of enslaved Africans to immobilize them (B 678) (30 August 1979. Photos by G. Kubik)

Danish firearm, as sold by slave traders to the king of Porto Seguro to suppress revolts. Family-owned from Hubert Kponton, Lomé (Togo), January 1970. Photo by G. Kubik.

A plate belonging to the Brazilian slave trader Francisco O. Silva from Porto Seguro (Togo), nineteenth century. Family-owned from Kponton, Lomé, January 1970. Photo by G. Kubik.

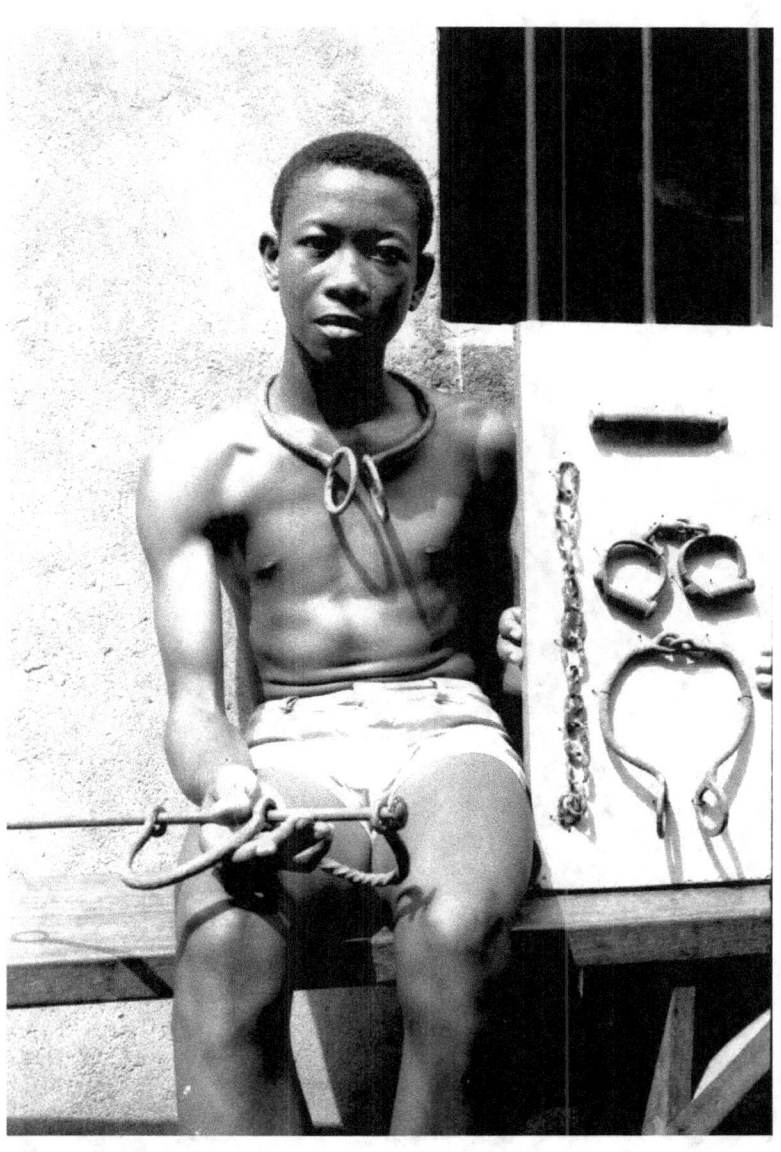

Instruments of slavery, family-owned from Hubert Kponton, Lomé. In this picture Kponton's nephew demonstrates the usage. Lomé, January 1970. Photo by G. Kubik.

The Slave House ("Maison des esclaves") on the Ile de Gorée near Dakar (Senegal), transit point for enslaved Africans from West Africa on their way to the Americas.

Today the "Maison des esclaves" is a museum. December 1981. Photos by G. Kubik (H 86, H 116).

On the other side of the Atlantic Ocean there was often a similar island on which a temporary transit camp for the deported Africans was located. For example, the Forte de São Marcelo in the Bay of Bahia (middle of photo), directly in front of the old market at the beach (today, in its renovated version, "Mercado Modelo"). Salvador/Bahia, October 1975. Photo by G. Kubik (B 776).

"Marché aux Nègres" (Negro Market), an important image by Johann Moritz Rugendas from Rio de Janeiro, 1835. The newly arrived Africans, divided into groups of men and women, sit or lie on mats, the women in front of a cooking fire, waiting to be sold. An exceptional observation by Rugandas shows one of these women (middle) stretching her hands in the direction of the fire underneath her cooking pot in a way that one calls kwota tuhya in East Angola. At left, a boy occupies himself—under the attentive watch of a smoking "Senhor"—by drawing on the wall as another boy watches. The sketches include a sailboat, various heads with European features and caracature-like exaggerated pointy noses—probably the slave trader on that boat—and in the background a helpless human figure with his arms stretched out. Reproduction from Johann Moritz Rugendas.

This illustration by Johann Moritz Rugendas, 1835, "Transport d'un convoy de Nègres," shows the next step in the slave trading process – the removal of the just-purchased enslaved Africans.

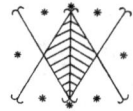

CULTURAL GROUPINGS AND AFRICAN-BRAZILIAN CULTURAL ZONES

It is difficult today to put one's finger on the old "ethnic" divisions of African populations in Brazil. Although the post-1888 ethnic identity of African-Brazilians became increasingly diluted, a hidden form still exists today. The earlier "nações" (nations) developed, often independently of any genealogy, into clearly delineated groups. In other words, "Nagô," "Angola," "Congo," and so on is still found in Brazil, although not always in any direct lineage. Extensions of specific African regional cultures—and not only in mixed form—persist today on Brazilian soil. For example, the cultures of the Nagô/Yorùbá in Bahia, the "Banguëla" in Minas Gerais, the Congo on the island São Sebastião off the coast of São Paulo, and in the town of Vila Bela da Santíssima Trindade in Mato Grosso—just to mention a few. Sometimes various cultural groupings exist alongside each other and in the same town. Experiencing this in a metropolis like Salvador/Bahia during my first trip to Brazil in 1974 was a completely unexpected shock (cf. Kubik 1979a, 13-22).

Cultural groups exist there for the most part independent of any "ethnic" background of their members. The cultural behavior of some Luso- Brazilians can be fairly influenced by aspects of Yorùbá cultural heritage. These individuals, for example, also actively participate in "candomblé" cultural events. For those European observers who come from a spiritual background in which "race" and "culture" are equated with one another, it can be a big surprise to see white participants in so-called African "demonic possession" rituals in Bahia—and it can be difficult to accept this as normal.

While the religious practices of the cult-groups in the city of Salvador/Bahia are dominated by elements of the Yorùbá religion, occasionally some Vodun (of the Fon of Dahomey), Bantu and Amerindian elements—and are marked by Catholicism—the heritage of Angola is evident in the streets and on the beaches. Countless members of *samba* street groups are influenced in their movements by the Angolan culture, without even knowing it.[16] Brazil is an instructive example of how culture can be learned.

Over the course of three centuries, regional neo-African cultures have developed. Although our current research is not exhaustive, it is possible at this point, amongst other things, to identify the following zones:

1. The culture of Bahia, with a high proportion of cultural elements from southwest Nigeria and Dahomey (Nagô/Yorùbá, Fon, Ewe, etc.), accompanied by a Congo/Angola element attributable to a secondary proliferation from the southern part of Brazil.

2. The culture of the region around Rio de Janeiro (Baixada Fluminense) with predominantly Angolan-area cultural elements.

3. The African cultural islands at the state of São Paulo, for example, the small town Capivari, on the island Ilhabela, in the area around Salto de Pirapora and in São Paulo itself. These are almost exclusively influenced by cultural elements from the Congo/Angola area and some elements from Mozambique.

4. The African cultural islands of Minas Gerais in which the majority of elements originated in the hinterland of Benguela in Angola.

5. African cultural islands in Brazil's interior, for example, in Mato Grosso, which displays mostly Congo elements. In addition, there are regions in the north (for example, Maranhão) which have been researched by the sociologist Kazadi wa Mukuna.

In all these aforementioned cultural areas various configurations of African heritage originated since, over time, selections, strengthening and dilution of African elements took place due to various Brazilian circumstances. That is to say, at various times and at different places in the new "home," one or the other cultural element was favored, while others were destined to disappear.

The African cultural elements in Brazil have manifested themselves in very diverse surroundings and socio-economic contexts. We can differentiate between:

1. *Urban African-Brazilian cultures.* Examples include Salvador/Bahia, Rio de Janeiro, and Recife.

2. *Small village communities* (former *senzalas*, "slave settlements") which support themselves with local agricultural products, although they are still economically dependent on the surrounding *fazendas*, land parcels belonging to regional owners. Examples of these communities include the Cafundó village near Salto de Pirapora, in the state of São Paulo, as well as three more (i.e., Caxambu, Pilar do Sul and Bairro de Fazendinha) nearby in the same region, though they have been dissolved. In this area, African cultural heritage continues to live on in village traditions.

3. *Family groups* of African descent in small cities which hand down traditions from one generation to the next; observe certain *folguedos* such as "Congada," "Maracatú," "Mozambique" or references such as *batuque* in dance. An example of all this is the Benedito Caxias family in Capivari.

4. *Riverside aggregations* whose size can range up to small cities or interconnected villages. Examples include XiqueXique on the São Francisco River in Bahia, where Guilherme dos Santos undertook wide-ranging studies; and Vila Bela da Santíssima Trindade (Mato Grosso) on the Guaporé River, where our research group worked in October/November 1980. In a certain respect the population centers on the coast, such as "Reconcavo" in Bahia, also fall into this category.

5. *Remote and isolated homesteads* or settlements, mostly in mountainous regions, regarded as successors of former *quilombos* or *mocambos*. Examples of such homesteads include settlements in the mountains near Quartel do Indaiá,

Minas Gerais.

There are many elements, above all, Brazil's urban cultures, which can be regarded as neo-African. That is, cultural manifestations which in their structure and contents are predominantly stamped by African cultures, but are nevertheless highly mutated forms. From an African perspective it must be said that a new regional African culture outside the African mainstream has established itself. The metropolitan *samba* culture is one example. Samba is not only a music and dance form, but also a lifestyle. In the meantime it has become so closely associated with a Brazilian national culture that even in Brazil its symbolism as a feature of African identity has disappeared amongst certain social groups. The *Movimento Negro* does not regard the samba lifestyle as a symbol of "African Consciousness" (Tiago de Oliveira Pinto 1986a,12-13).

The Brazilian music and dance form called *samba* first emerged in writing in the 3 February 1838 edition of the newspaper *O Carapuceiro*, Pernambuco. African-Brazilian dances in the early nineteenth century had generally been referred to as "baducca," "batuca," "batuque," etc. It is likely that the word *samba* had been utilized earlier in *batuque* performances to describe a type or order of specialized movements; it was later, however, perhaps when the typical *samba* motions had become particularly fashionable, that the word *samba* was widely used and became synonymous with an autonomous dance style.

Dance traditions called *samba* which had perhaps been known earlier by other names continued to split into countless specific dance formations during the following century. By that time they were known as *samba*. Today "samba-de-roda" and its circular formation is the most well-known form found in Recòncavo Baiano (the Bahian sugar cane cultivation region). This is not an urban form. Other significant designations for *samba* types are "samba de umbigada," "samba-de-chula," "samba-de-viola," etc.[17] In addition to these and many other designations are those by which specific forms of urban *samba* are categorized regionally: for example, "samba carioca," the *samba* from Rio de Janeiro which has become world renowned thanks to the annual February Mardi Gras festivities. In Rio de Janeiro the term "bossa nova" has been used since the end of the fifties for a type of *samba* music performed in concert and characterized by jazz harmonies from the North American jazz tradition and with a particular emphasis on lyrics. This "bourgeois" form of *samba* was rarely practiced by African-Brazilian musicians. The nomenclature itself originated in the recording industry.

A number of opinions have been expressed about the etymology of the Brazilian term *samba*. The majority of authors are unanimous that the name comes from Africa. Our own research on this topic has revealed the following insights. A Bantu-language origin is likely given the phonology, in particular the presence of the homo-organic "mb" sound as in "rumba," used in the Afro-Cuban area. A root word *-samba* exists in numerous Bantu languages found all the way from Angola and Congo to East Africa (Luganda) as the verb *kusamba*, albeit with very different meanings. In Cinyanja (the language of the Maravi ethnic groups of southeast Africa), *kusamba* means "to wash oneself." In the Luganda language (southern Uganda), there is a song titled *Bijjabisamba endege* ("they who come stomping with rattles on their feet"). It is evident that the root word, *samba,* where it exists in most Bantu languages, refers to a procedure of motion. When seeking a correlation of the Brazilian expression with the African one, one cannot overlook the fact that the Bantu languages are tonal ones. So one must always ask, is the semantic pronunciation *sámba* or *sàmba*? Comparable African concepts are found in words with a falling tone, in this case *sàmba*.

For various other reasons and above all based on musical evidence, the only source for the Brazilian term *samba* is Angola or the most southern part of Congo.[18] Several Brazilian authors have also correctly honed in on that region. It had been suggested that the word was derived from the Kimbundu language (Luanda, Angola) word *semba*. This concept was also applied to the "umbigada"—the bumping together of partners' bellies, which also appear in the Brazilian *samba*—in the framework of *rebita* dance clubs in Luanda.[19] For reasons of phonology, however, this derivation is improbable. *Semba* contains an open e-sound; in Brazilian pronunciation, however, *samba* has a nasal ã. It would have to be a Bantu source word like *samba*, with a pure [a] that accounts for the Brazilian nasalization.

Through arduous and exacting work we were able to compile some additional data from Angola. A verb *kusamba* exits in the languages of the Ngangela group in precisely that region of East Angola in which an important rhythmic attribute of Brazilian *samba* music originated. This is the so-called sixteen-pulse timeline pattern.[20] My interview subject Mose Yotamu, who lives in northwest Zambia near the Angolan border, and whose indigenous tongue is Luvale, gave this example using the word meaning "hop" or "jump" in the Ngangela groups' language: *vambambi vekusamba ngwe kuli kalunga wamundende* (the antelopes jump when drizzle is on its way).[21] This subject is also familiar with dance movements identified with the suffix *samba* from this cultural realm. Much earlier, on 6 September 1971, he told me that there is a very old dance style characterized by side-to-side shoulder movements, called *ndembendembe ya samba*. Later he mentioned a "very old dance" of the Luvale in East Angola called *samba-kalata*.[22]

The verb *kusamba* is translated in Emil Pearson's *Ngangela-English Dictionary* (1970) as "skip, gambol," as an expression of overflowing joy. *Samba* is also used as a person's name in Angola and other Bantu language areas of Africa. In one of the oldest cultural institutions of East Angola, the *mukanda* circumcision school, a song with the text "Samba papelo, viyaya vyovyo ..." has been passed down through the generations. The text is so old that it can no longer be translated. Here, Samba is possibly a person's name. This song is sung at night and accompanied by the boys of the initiation school and their male guardians striking concussion sticks (*mingongi*), similar to the sticks used in the Brazilian *maculelê*.[23]

The filmmaker António Paulo de Oliveira from Angola told me in a conversation on 14 January 1981 in Luanda that the word *samba* is used to mean "clap hands" in Gabela (Povoção do Assango) in the province of Kwanza-Sul—that is, *kusamba apando*, or *bater palmas* ("clap hands"), as is done in ceremonial greetings.

We cannot yet reconstruct in detail the origin of the concept *samba* in a Brazilian context. However, the large volume of data now available from the Angolan cultural sphere points to Angolan origin of both the music and dance movements as well as the word *samba*. It is a result of normal historical processes of divergent development that both elements underwent changes in form as well as meaning in the Americas.

The influence of urbanization on the processes of innovation in Brazil may not be underestimated. The most significant cultural innovations from the middle of the nineteenth century onwards most likely stemmed from urban areas. Parts of the rural countryside, however, remained cultural withdrawal areas in which historical forms lived on. Due to the huge wave of migration moving from rural areas, especially the northeast part of the country, to the industrial cities São Paulo and Rio de Janeiro in the south, a metropolitan population of tremendous cultural-innovation energy developed. Today about two-thirds of the total Brazilian population live in the cities.

The areas of population concentration in Brazil were fertile ground supporting the further existence of African religions. To a certain extent they existed in almost unaltered form such as the Yorùbá *candomblés* using Yorùbá as the liturgical language, with Salvador/Bahia as the most important center. Exactly why Salvador was such favorable ground for the transplantation of a Yorùbá culture can be explained by the predominantly Nagô (Yorùbá) demographic amongst the enslaved Africans of the most recent period and the fact that the Yorùbá and other cultures from the coast of West Africa displayed a remarkably cosmopolitan character.[24] This led to the establishment of an African-influenced urban culture most strongly seen in the Brazilian urban centers, specifically where there was a sufficient prevalence of Yorùbá members and speakers.

In the rural area of Bahia the Yorùbá cultural influence is not nearly as predominant as in and around the former Brazilian capital. This statement foreshadows a theory to be introduced later that transplanted cultures display the tendency to preferably set down new roots in those places where the ecological and social conditions are most similar to those of their place of origin.

In respect to their African heritage, the Brazilian city cultures have been relatively well investigated. Countless names come to mind in connection with the study of the Yorùbá culture, above all regarding religious manifestations, in Bahia.[25] Despite the relatively thorough research of the Yorùbá cultural sector in Bahia, every once in a while unexpected discoveries are still made, in particular as it appears, in the less-penetrated adjacent regions like Pernambuco. My Brazilian colleague José Jorge de Carvalho discovered Yorùbá drums called *bàtá* several years ago in Recife (Pernambuco). In this context, I quote here from his letter to me from 2 August 1976 (from Caracas, Venezuela):

> I recorded all the songs and rhythms and attended to almost all the ceremonies of the Nagô nation of the *Xangos*, the Afro-Brazilian religious group as found today in Recife, State of Pernambuco. The Nagô is the orthodox group, still singing in Yorùbá language as the candomblés in Bahia ... I think my collection is the first complete one ever made of this Afro-American religious group. Even in Bahia (and you please correct me if I am wrong) I wonder if they have made anything better than the old Herskovits's collection, recorded at Bahia, 1942. I found in a Nagô religous house in Recife a trio of double-skin drums called *bàtá*, played hung around the neck, completely unknown before in the Afro-Brazilian studies.

Since then Carvalho completed and published excerpts from his doctorate on this subject.[26]

Even during the era of slavery the urban conditions in Brazil were quite different from plantation life. Johann Moritz Rugendas delivered an eloquent report about the city of Rio de Janeiro in the first half of the nineteenth century, a city whose population majority—in contrast to Bahia—comprised people from the Bantu area of Africa.

> A large part of the slave population of Rio de Janeiro live as house servants of prominent rich people. They are regarded as a luxury article, one determined more by the vanity of the master than the needs of the household. These slaves wear Francish uniforms, mostly quite antiquated in style, and, together with the matching wigs, presents quite a caricature. They have little or nothing to do, are well-fed, and, to put it succinctly, are almost as superfluous as the ser-

vants in the grand homes of Europe—and they are just as accustomed to debauchment too. Most of the slaves in larger cities do have to pay their master on a daily or weekly basis; a certain sum that they earn by doing various handiworks: as carpenters, shoemakers, tailors, boat-hands, manual laborers, etc. In this situation they can easily earn more than their master demands from them, and if such a slave lives fairly sparingly, it cannot be very difficult to buy his own freedom in nine to ten years.

However, this doesn't happen as often as one might think, since the Negroes tend to waste their money terribly, and throw away everything they earn, particularly on clothes, colorful scarves and ribbons.

Since they go about their business freely every day and only come home in the evening, and their masters only pay attention to them to the extent that they collect their weekly payment, the slaves enjoy much freedom, and, all in all, a quite tolerable existence. Before they leave the house in the morning, and when they return in the evening, they receive tapioca and beans. During the day they have to find their own food. In the same way, many women slaves earn their keep as nurses, laundresses, flower- and fruit-sellers, etc (Rugendas 1835, 17-18).

Almost 180 years after Rugendas and some 120 years after abolition of slavery, the leisurely lifestyle in the Rio de Janeiro still display elements reminiscent of that time. For example, the unofficial ideal of beauty inherited from the time of slavery, the *mulata*, African girls whose light skin attests to the comingling of the *senhor*'s race; or the culture of ice cream and drink vendors at the beach who often drum *samba* rhythms on their containers; or the flower sellers; or the shoeshine boys. It is astounding how much was passed on from the past century within the cultural pockets of Rio de Janeiro.[27] Many elements from Rio de Janeiro's social climate and elaborate costume traditions of the nineteenth century re-appear annually at Carnival at the end of

February.

On the plantations, the families of the *senhor* and the enslaved Africans lived in separate residential buildings: "casa grande" (the master's house) and "senzala" (slave quarters).[28] Rugandas made another interesting observation regarding the division of land:

> On every plantation there is a relatively large section of land which the owner does not use, but leaves to the slaves to cultivate as much as each one desires or can. The harvest from these fields not only supplies sufficient and nutritious food, it also can be sold, to a slave's great advantage...
>
> Negroes who are freed from the plantations generally settle near the crops that they previously oversaw as slaves, and cultivate a small field which is often provided by their previous master at a minimal lease or even no cost.[29]

This is the historical background of the origin of small, isolated village communities stamped with an African character, mostly at low elevations, with access to flowing water, and surrounded by the *fazendas* of former masters and, today, big land owners. After abolition in 1888 the slave groups stayed on the property that their owners had designated for their cultivation. Sometimes the land was formally transferred to them via a certificate. (Occasionally such certificates were preserved in the archives by the prefectures.)

One example of such a village is Bairro do Cafundó, a small rural community of about 70 people, only 15 kilometers from the city of Salto de Pirapora and about 140 km from São Paulo. In April/May 1979, as well as October/November 1980, I did concentrated work here together with Guilherme dos Santos Barbosa, São Paulo, and in 1980 with both my African colleagues Kachamba and Moya.

At first sight Cafundó, with its square, grass-covered mud houses, banana stalks, corn and peanut fields, rice patties near a small stream and clean sandy ground, evoked an impression of an Angolan village somewhere in the eastern part of Angola. The ancestors of the present settlement were predominantly Angolans. It is probable that the majority were sold into this area as enslaved Africans as late as the eighteenth century to work for the land owners.

In the environs of Salto de Pirapora as little as about twenty years ago, there were still four such villages with populations of Angolan descent (i.e., Cafundó, Caxambu, Pilar do Sul and Bairro de Fazendinha) that were not isolated persons, but rather groups continuing a retention of their own culture under the leadership of a village chief (in local terminology of the prefecture: "lider" [leader]). Only Cafundó, however, remains today. The other three villages were dissolved one after the other in the past few years (two cases through illegal manipulations by the large land owners), and the residents were driven into the cities.[30] At the "Intercongress" of the International Union of Anthropological and Ethnological Sciences (IUAES) in Amsterdam (April 22-25, 1981), this was the topic of a talk by Guilherme dos Santos Barbosa. He also wrote a letter to "Survival International," London, with the request that intervention take place.[31]

During his talk, dos Santos Barbosa examined the meaning of the word "cafundó." He highlighted interesting differences between the meanings in Brazilian, Portuguese and the concept as understood by the village residents. He noted:

> According to information collected from Mr. Silvino Pires Pedroso, this community was formerly called Barra. But gradually another name came up—one does not know how—which competed with the former one and would apply to a rather vast portion of that sandy terrain: that name was Cafundó; it was already given to that land by their forbears while they were still captives, the ancestors of the present-day community. Thereafter, the place became generally known as Cafundó da Barre. The power of this term was already felt during that period...
>
> In order to clarify the etymology of that name given to the community, we also consulted the Dictionário Enciclopédico Brasileiro Ilustrado which was compiled under the direction of Professor Alvaro Gui-

marães and published by the Livraria Globo in 1947. There we find: Cafundó – m., a flat terrain, surrounded by steep and high hills; a remote place, difficult to reach, normally situated between mountains; a dark place in a house.... In another, small dictionary of the Portuguese language we find: Cafundós – sm., pl., distant and unknown places.... But the inhabitants of Cafundó gave me the following definition: Cafundó – a place that is low, fenced in by hills....[32]

Whether the word "cafundó" (pronounced *kafundo*) could possibly be an old Portuguese/Brazilian borrowed word from a Bantu language has not yet been proven with any certainty.

Angolan cultural heritage in Bairro do Cafundó was still very evident in 1980 in the following areas: (a) traditional technique of building construction; (b) handicrafts, for example, basket-making; (c) political-social organization (existence of a typical "soba," Sr. Otávio Caetano, app. 60 years old, with the function of justice administration); (d) organization of agricultural work;[33] (e) children's games, for example, boys using a gourd to make the form of a cow (*ongombe*); f) oral literature; and (g) songs and playing of percussion instruments. In addition, there are many less obvious examples, from the way in which an orange is peeled to how a pit trap is made to catch the despised *fazenda*-owner's roaming cow that jumped the fence onto the property of a Cafundó resident. The trap-builder left a tiny hole in the middle of the floating surface of the pit trap, and intentionally removed the section of compromised fence. Verney Lovett Cameron (1885) reported exactly the same thing from his trip to the Luvale in the region of the Upper Zambezi:

> We reached a village of about twenty dwellings, in the middle of a large enclosure; and whilst climbing over the fence at what appeared to be a proper entrance, I heard people call out 'Take care! There's a hole!' I looked at the ground most carefully, and, avoiding a small hole, placed my foot on what seemed a remarkably sound spot. Immediately the surface gave way, and I made a rapid descent into a pitfall for game... (Cameron 1885, 405).

Most surprising in Cafundó, however, is that people still remember the "African language" (*a língua africana*) of the ancestors. Displaced residents of the dissolved settlements also still remember it, as our interview with the *lider* (leader) of Caxambu, Sr. Emiliano confirmed.[34] In the meantime the language has shrunk down to around maximum 200 to 300 lingistic terms—despite this, impressive "conversations" can still be held.[35] Based on my research since 1979, the vocabulary of Cafundó is mainly comprised of Umbundu, Kimbundu and a smaller proportion of Kikoongo, Songo, Ngangela, Luvale and Lundaelements.[36]

African heritage is preserved, so to speak, in the side streets and courtyards. Capivari is a small city in the state of São Paulo, about 100 km from São Paulo via Itú. The total population has markedly fewer people of African descent than in the past. Several African-Brazilian families live in one of the streets near the small Capivari River, including the extended family of Sr. Benedito Caxias.[37] In 1979 Caxias was "Chefe da Sociedade de Batuque Capivariano" (the head of the Batuque Society of Capivari), a traditional organization which passes down the *batuque* dance tradition to his own family members and a selected group of students.

In the nineteenth century, African dance forms existent in Brazil were lumped together by Luso-Brazilians under the concept of *batuque* (Cascudo 1954). Batuque is often mixed up with "batucada," a type of ensemble of various percussion instruments with no traditional African origin. Batuque groups using traditional drums built in African style may still be found today in a few places in the state of São Paulo. In a suburb of São Paulo there is a *batuque* association well known to folklore researcher Haydee Nascimento.

In the small city of Capivari in São Paulo state, 82-year old Benedito Caxias was safeguarding the valuable African-style drums built for *batuque* dance in the rear courtyard of his house when we visited him in 1979: *tambú*, the bottomless, deep-toned single-skinned lead drum; "quinjengue" (written in Bantu orthography: *kinjenge*), a smaller cup-shaped drum with an acoustic hole on the side and a long, toothlike supporting leg, used to play accompaniment; *matraca*, two percussive sticks with which a musician struck the floor-standing *tambú* in a time-line pattern; and finally, a double-cone tin rattle (similar to those in the Umbanda religious practices) called *guaiá*.

Benedito Caxias still remembered the area of his grandparents' African origin. His grandfather and grandmother on his father's side, Manoel Caxias and Ana Maria Caxias, came from the "Costa da Africa," with which he probably meant the West African coast. His grandparents on his mother's side, Tobias Francisco da Cruz and Jacinta da Cruz, came from Mozambique.

Caxias's *batuque* drum-playing is based on the heritage of African traditions from Mozambique and the Congo/Angola area, in arrangements and re-interpretations of march rhythms originating in the Luso-Brazilian environment of the nineteenth century.[38] The structural features of the two drums point towards the same direction of Africa. The type of cup-shaped drum he called "quinjengue" with the very long support leg is only found in Southeast Africa, in the area between the Ruvuma Valley, Lake Malawi and the Zambezi Valley. The most comparable instrument to the "quinjengue" can be found amongst the collection of several instruments of this type kept in the Museu de Etnologia, Lisboa, a drum acquired in the vicinity of Tete, Mozambique.[39] The name "quinjengue" (*kinjenge*), however, points to a different area of Africa—to southwest Angola, to the OvaNkhumbi, OvaHanda and OvaCilenge, where there are drums with a similar sounding name *kenjengo*.[40] The lead drum *tambú*, in its construction and playing method (positioning and use of little sticks to beat a time-line rhythm, e.g. the eight-pulse pattern [x..x..x.]), points towards the North Angola/lower Congo region. The name *tambú*, in one or the other language variations, is common with the Mpangu, a Bakoongo-subgroup in western Congo.[41] The double-coned rattle made of tin can also be found here, but it is called *nsaka*.[42] The term *guaiá*, or *xakwayo* in the remaining African vocabulary of the village Cafundó, widely recognized in Brazil's south, show connections to the terms for "rattle" in North Angola.

The example of Benedito Caxias's *batuque* demonstrates, on the one hand, the intensity of transculturation between various African traditions (in this case, Bantu) in nineteenth century Brazil, and the unexpected configurations it generated. It also points to modifications and changes in the semantic scope of vocabulary with origins in Africa. As our recordings show, a neo-African tradition rooted itself in the soil of the Americas as a sort of "extended family."

Quite a bit of verbal culture (stories, riddles, etc.) gets passed down in large-family environments of African descent. Vicente dos Santos, born in 1954, was one of my interlocutors during my Bahia field research in 1974 and 1975. An orphan, he spent his childhood with his guardian grandmother in Santa Rosa de Lima, about 50 kilometers outside Salvador. Vicente felt a strong connection to the elderly woman who, according to African tradition, commanded an important position in the household. When his grandmother died in 1976, Vicente wanted to leave Brazil for Africa: "Minha avó morreu e estou muito triste, agora sou só quero ir para Africa com Donald Cachamba e seus irmãos...." (My grandmother died and I am very sad, [and] now I just want to go to Africa with Donald Kachamba and his brothers).[43] Thanks to his grandmother, he was acquainted with countless stories containing African words and imagery, such as "cacimba de baixo."[44] In the East Angola languages *lisima* is a well, *kasima*, a small well. Further to the west the pronunciation is often *kasimba*. In Vicente's African-Bahian tradition, "cacimba" (*kasimba*) means a spring, or a watering-spot where women wash clothes (*fonte onde as mulheres lavam roupa*); "cacimba de baixo" therewith means the little watering-place down (there).

His grandmother's stories, as told by Vicente dos Santos, are almost direct translations from African stories into Brazilian, with complete retention of their original structure. They belong to a genre of African tales peppered with song, which appears at dramatic points. African animal figures like the toad (Portuguese: *sapo*) or the turtle (Portuguese: *cágado*) play a major role in many of these stories.[45] Two African traditions—the one Angola, the other Nigerian—have probably reinforced one another in the tortoise stories in Bahia. In East Angola and neighboring areas there are countless stories in which *mbati* or *suwangongo* (Ngangela language group) appear as trickster-figures with the hare (*kalumba*).[46] Here, as in the African-Bahian tales of Vicente's grandmother, it is a freshwater turtle that is emphasized in a very conspicuous way by Vicente. Cágado ("cágo" for short) is not the same as *tartaruga*, which lives in salt water. In the

Yorùbá àló tales, which I thoroughly documented in Oshogbo and neighboring towns in West Nigeria in 1960 and 1963, àhún, the land-based tortoise, is in fact the most important trickster figure there is.

An interesting occurrence in this African-Bahian oral tradition is that occasionally some phrases in the Brazilian version, in particular formulaic passages, are created from a so-called phonemic transfer of whole phrases or word clusters from the original African languages. A few African items or word combinations (which the Portuguese-speaking listener of the original versions of these tales could not make out) are retained as "texted Africanisms" and take on onomatopoeic or rhythmic functions in the Brazilian story versions. The unusual word patterns can be seen in a story by Vicente dos Santos. "Tá no pé de bobê! Tá no pé de bobê! Oi cadê meu facão? Tá no pé de bobê! Oi cadê meu facão? Tá no pé de bobê!"[47] This formula appears at a moment of high drama, when the man in the story comes home and surprises his wife who is together with another man. He yells, "Oi! Where is my bush-knife?" To distract him and get him out of the house, the woman answers, "It's in the pumpkin plant!" (Literally, it is in the foot of the pumpkin). Although this established wording makes sense in a Brazilian context ("bobê" is a corrupted form of *abóbora*, "pumpkin"), these short, rhythmically spoken monosyllabic sequences with nasal qualities and tonality (!) are so reminiscent of Yorùbá that it wouldn't surprise me if a Yorùbá speaker would be able to transcribe this back into his language. Guilherme dos Santos Barbosa, who transcribed Vicente's texts in May 1981, said of this established wording that it is spoken in the manner of a "preto velho," a figure of the old, indigenous-enslaved Africans, now of mythological status.

The population centers on the large rivers, like along the Rio São Francisco in Bahia or in the city Vila Bela da Santíssima Trindade on the Guaporé River near the Bolivian border, resulted, in cases of predominantly African descendants, in unique fluvial cultures of African character. Fishing always plays a large economic role along these rivers, and parallel to this, there are religious traditions and ideas that are connected with the river. Guilherme dos Santos Barbosa, who investigated the religious ideas of the population in his hometown Xique-Xique on the Rio

São Francisco, told me about a strange place of "spirits" which the people in his area call *mocambo do vento* (hiding place of the wind). This is a very windy spot on the river near Xique-Xique where there are many stones in the water. This is a very dangerous place to navigate for ships both large and small.

Guilherme related to me that people residing on the banks of rivers often have a mystical relationship with strong current—a feeling which they themselves cannot explain. Guilherme, despite living in São Paulo since childhood, cannot escape this bond. On our travels together in October/November in the Mato Grosso, Guilherme had the habit of stopping his Volkswagen at every large river en route and spending at least an hour there before he felt himself mentally prepared to continue the journey. My colleagues from an African highlands area had little appreciation for this. They felt most at home in a village atmosphere where they could wander around on foot, like in Cafundó. And I myself felt most inclined during the trip to Mato Grosso to set up our camping site far from any residential areas.

Following my stay in Brazil, I sent Guilherme a postcard of the Kwanza River, where I was doing field work in the village of Kalumbu during my January 1981 trip to Angola. He wrote back to me on 17 February 1981:

> I would like to express the intense feelings that were overwhelming me when I received your postcard showing the Kwanza river, a precise resemblance of the daily experience of my beloved city of Xique-Xique with my river, São Francisco, and my people. If God allows me, I would still want to carry out research in those regions of Africa that have some relationship with our history. I was gazing at that postcard for a long time, it was telling me much... and it is interesting how you [in Portuguese he addressed me politely in the third person] seem to know me and touch me at the point where I am most vulnerable, spiritually.

The culture of Vila Bela de Santíssima Trindade, former capital city of Mato Grosso with a population dominated by people of African descent, is an interesting case. I could not ascertain the city's exact number of residents; I estimated it, however, at 7,000 to 8,000. The city was founded when gold was discovered in this region in the eighteenth century, resulting in a heavy influx into Mato Grosso of so-called "bandeirantes" (from the Portuguese *bandeira*, "flag"), a hodgepodge of adventurers, prospectors, slave-hunters, etc. Soon after this, slave labor was needed to exploit the gold mines. These enslaved Africans were delivered from other parts of Brazil, and thus constitute a secondary proliferation of African population elements. Opinions diverge as to the exact origin of the slave laborers. Sergio Coelho, a journalist from Sorocaba, the state of São Paulo, who has been dealing with Brazil's African peoples for several years, is of the view that the slave laborers were brought to Mato Grosso from São Paulo.

> Taken from São Paulo to Mato Grosso, the enslaved Africans were used for work in the mines, during the era of open exploration. With the end of slavery and the exhaustion of the mineral deposits these black contingents—possibly in an attempt to return to their original fluvial life-styles—installed themselves at the banks of the Guaporé river, where the town of Vila Bela is found today....[48]

Guilherme dos Santos Barbosa is of a completely different opinion: the penetration of Mato Grosso did not take place from São Paulo, but rather from the northwest, along the Guaporé River. "The *senhores* brought the enslaved Africans in boats along the Rio Guaporé," he said.[49]

The economic boom of the city of Vila Bela did not last long; however there are still traces of this golden era in the ruins of the large cathedral, the *palácio*, and other buildings. The gold mines are dormant and, practically speaking, only accessible via a small aircraft since an approximately 70-kilometer-long stretch of the land route is completely overgrown.

The exodus from Vila Bela began following the depletion of the gold mines. According to a detail that Guilherme dos Santos Barbosa received from Sr. Paulo Roberto Marine during our stay at the end of October/beginning of November 1980, the African-Brazilian population of this town dwindled to just two permanently-settled black families. Almost all of today's inhabitants are descended from these two families, says the interviewee. As a result they are all also related to each other.

A fluvial culture of Central African character established itself here in the following period, during which borrowings from the Amerindian population facilitated the restoration of an African heritage. In some respects Vila Bela is reminiscent of an old abandoned trading post of the type found along large rivers in the Congo area on the Congo River or its estuaries. This impression as we walked along the Guaporé was not only my personal one, but most significantly, was shared by my colleagues who had made the long journey from Africa. Our *déjà-vu* experiences were anything but subtle: the *pirogues*; the Congo-style haircutting under large shady trees by the river; the "Congada" or "Festa de Congo," which takes place each year around 15 October in Vila Bela, and at which a "King of the Congo" (*rei do Congo*) is chosen.

Our interview with the head of the Congada, Sr. Urbano Fernando de Leite (male, 39 years old) in Vila Bela, uses dense clusters of African, probably predominantly Kikoongo words, in a Portuguese text.[50] This became apparent to us only after dos Santos Barbosa transcribed the text. The evidently prevalent Congo element in Vila Bela's culture also popped up in a *roda* (round dance) performed one evening by six- to fourteen-year-old children, mostly girls, accompanied by singing and clapping.[51] Discrete forms of Central African concepts were also evident on All Souls Day (*Dia de finados*) at the Vila Bela Catholic Cemetery, engulfed by an indescribable sea of light from memorial candles on the evening of November 2. These candles were set up just centimeters apart on the gravesites, and, in particular, around the giant cross directly inside the entrance to the cemetery. The procession and the intuitively perceptible cloak of meaning in which the ritual was shrouded reminded me of a region of Africa, that of the *bwiti* religious practices in Gabon, with which I became acquainted while there in 1964 and 1966. My African associates Moya and Kachamba had a different reaction to this ceremony – one of terror, that the sea of light at the cemetery was to be interpreted as an evil omen. Both balked at entering, and only did so when encouraged by an elderly woman. One of them would under no circumstances walk around the light-engulfed cross at the entrance, as did all the other visitors from the city.

African population elements have also penetrated the Amerindian population around Vila Bela. As we traveled from Diceres to Vila Bela we photographed groups of children of African appearance with noticeable Amerindian features in front of palm-leaf- roofed clay dwellings. In Vila Bela itself, Amerindian families live in wooden houses on the left bank of the Guaporé while the city itself on the right bank is populated almost exclusively by people of African descent, as well as a few Luso-Brasilians who work in administrative or commercial occupations.

In a certain respect the population centers on the Brazilian coast, particularly the Recôncavo Baiano, the densely inhabited bay south of the city Salvador/Bahia, are also comparable to the "fluvial cultures." If not assigning them to a specially-created category for maritime cultures and settlements, these would most appropriately be classified in our Group 4. In contrast to the small village communities they have a wider territorial expanse and hold a middle position between rural and urban cultural forms. The Recôncavo sugar cane region is characterized by dense settlement, small towns resulting from the agglomerations and a strong relationship to large bodies of water (in this case, the ocean and its feeders).

Minas Gerais was one of the regions of Brazil in which the discovery of gold and diamonds from 1693 onwards resulted in an eighteenth-century influx of enslaved African population elements. In the former mining area around the structurally and architecturally well-preserved city Diamantina, north of Belo Horizonte, there is a range of African cultural islands whose residents are ancestors of earlier mine workers as well as, to a certain extent, scattered former *quilombos* from the mountainous region of Minas Gerais.

The expression "quilombo" comes from the Kimbundu and related languages of Angola. *Kilombo* (pl. *ilombo*) in Kimbundu, *ocilombo* (pl. *ovilombo*) in Umbundu and *chilombo* (pl. *vilombo*) in the Ngangela languages of East Angola refer to a temporary camp in the woods or the wilderness, specifically, one erected by hunters who stay out overnight, or, in more recent Angolan history, guerrilla groups. The opposite of *kilombo* is a permanent settlement, a village. In Brazil the expression has taken on the meaning "settlement of escaped enslaved Africans."

In Brazilian literature *quilombos* describes in a broader sense the settlements of escaped enslaved Africans which developed in the seventeenth and eighteenth centuries into state entities. The most famous of these *quilombos* was Palmares, an African state on Brazilian soil. Palmares included parts of the modern-day states Alagoas and Pernambuco and consisted of numerous smaller and larger settlements on rivers and in mountainous areas. The word Palmares means "palm trees," a reference to the local vegetation. It appears that Palmares was established around 1605-6, possibly even earlier (Kent 1973, 175). For almost a hundred years it retained its independence and withstood all Portuguese punitive efforts.

The population of Palmares was heterogeneous. It was evidently comprised of mostly Bantu-speaking groups as indicated by the name of one of their rulers, "Ganga-Zumba" (*Nganga-Zumba*), as well as a range of local terminology which, as in Africa, points back to personal names of chiefs; for example: "Andalaquituche" (probably Kimbundu: *Ndala-Kituxi*). *Ndala* means "the first-born." *Kituxi* is a person's name still used in Luanda today. *Nganga* has various meanings in the different languages of Angola. In Kikoongo the expression means "indigenous healer" in a positive sense. In the province Kwanza Norte, in the Dihunga language for instance, there is an additional meaning, roughly the concept of an *nganga-longo* (circumciser) in a *dilongo*, a traditional circumcision school.[52] "Among the Ovimbundu, however, the *onganga* is the magician who is evil and does evil."[53]

The dwellings of Palmares and other freed African settlements in Brazil were also often called *mocambos*, from the Kimbundu *mukambo*, "hiding place" (Mendonça 1935, 220). In the related language Umbundu *okambo* means "little settlement," "farmhouse," "homestead," and it is in this sense that the Brazilian adaptation *mocambo* is still used by many African-Brazilians in Bahia and Minas Gerais today.[54] The etymology of the Kimbundu and Umbundu terms is interesting since the root *-imbo* is present in both expressions. This root means "village" or "human settlement" in most of the Angolan languages, for instance *limbo* (pl. *membo*) in the languages of the Ngangela group of East Angola. A. Hauenstein, who lived amongst the Ovimbundu of Central Angola for 25 years, told me that *okambo*, is written correctly *okaimbo*, the exact translation of which is "small settlement."[55] The syllable *-ka* is most likely to be interpreted as a diminutive prefix in all variations of this word, yielding in Umbundu *O-ka-imbo* (starting vowel + diminutive prefix + root) translating to "the + small + settlement." Spoken quickly it becomes simply *okambo* as in the dictionary spelling.

Up into the nineteenth century there were many *quilombos* and (smaller) *mocambos* in relatively inaccessible mountainous regions of Brazil, particularly in the state of Minas Gerais. The structure of such installations can still be seen in the pattern of local settlements today, as in the mountains northwest of the city of Diamantina. There I documented numerous *quilombo-* or *mocambo*-like homesteads in the mountains and hills around the village Quartel do Indaiá in May 1979.

Aires da Mata Machado Filho undertook the first ethnological exploration in this region in 1928, in which he researched the *vissungos* (songs of labor), sung in the "lingua de Banguëla" in the town of S. João da Chapada near Diamantina. In his 1943 book, he cites the following *quilombos* in the vicinity around São João da Chapada:

> Around the place where the town of S. João da Chapada is found today, there were six famous 'quilombos': Caiambolas, Maquemba, one near the gorge of Formiga, the 'quilombo' of Antônio Moange, in Valvina, near the hill of Macumbá, one in Madalena and another one in the territory of the Fazenda of Bezerra.
>
> Geographical reasons, which oral tradition seems to confirm, let us believe that the population of Quartel de Indaiá, a curious community at nine kilometers from S. João da Chapada, came principally from those 'quilombos' first cited (Machado Filho 1943, 54).

My own visit to Quartel do Indaiá in May 1979 came about thanks to the kind intervention of Professor Romeu Sabará from the Departamento de Sociologia e Antropologia of the University of Minas Gerais, Belo Horizonte. He personally drove me there and brought me to the family of the store owner Pedro

Ninfa. My first impression of Quartel was rather disappointing. Absolutely no African cultural elements appeared evident. Quartel do Indaiá is a small village with very few houses, one single store and a small chapel. The residents make their living from stock-breeding – cows and horses. I only made some surprising discoveries after I managed to persuade two boys, about 10 and 14 years old (José Robinson Ferreira of Luso-Brazilian parentage and Adenilson Santos of African-Brazilian parentage) to help me as guides on my treks into the mountains and hills. On 8 May 1979 they led me to a peculiar settlement only about 1 kilometer away from Quartel; however, it seemed to be completely hidden. For me it was like a giant leap through a map of time and space in a science fiction story: suddenly I found myself, at the end of a path, on an African homestead. The photo documentation speaks for itself. In the middle of the smoothly swept plaza was a large square clay house covered with palm fronds. It had several rooms and two entrances, one on each side, that were connected by an interior corridor. The three inhabitants included a middle-aged man and two older women, one of them with a considerable goiter and taking deep drags on a *cachimbo*. Adjacent to the house there was an old sugar cane press and to my surprise, to the side of the house, a sort of shelter with a protective roof made of palm fronds and similar to the men's gathering spots in Angola (*ndzango* or *zango*). Here, however, this shelter also functioned as a coffee kitchen, and the women hospitably immediately offered me coffee made with sugar cane water. The homestead was surrounded by small corn fields, coffee groves and several banana trees and castor-oil plants. I was struck by the fact that amongst these African descendants there was no cow- and horse-raising like in Quartel.

Gradually I discovered many such homesteads in the surrounding hills and mountains in which family units lived separately from each another. The old *quilombos* had been concealed in the woods and hills. If one imagined that the navigable track from Diamantina via Sopa and São João da Chapada to Quartel do Indaiá, Várgem do Cural and Ponte Queimada were not there, then this alpine world, thickly wooded in many places, would be pretty much inaccessible. Fugitive enslaved Africans could best ensure their freedom by building isolated homesteads one or more kilometers away from the next one in this fairly inaccessible terrain. Since these settlements were scattered over a large area, they were, practically speaking, unconquerable. During the time of slavery there was probably a warning system set up amongst these free settlements.

This type of settlement still exists today. We walked along the footpaths to the more remote houses to interview the inhabitants, and above all to find out more about the "língua Banguëla." The material culture was still strongly characterized everywhere by Angolan elements. For the most part, the types of housing reflected the North Angolan square house style; women used mortars and pestles not to mash manioc or corn, but, interestingly enough, coffee. There was the typical structure behind some houses on which cooking pots or food intended for drying were placed or spread out, what we call *vutala* in East Angola. Some of my slides from Minas Gerais which I later showed during lecture trips at African universities elicited astonishment from the viewers. The students were convinced that these pictures were taken in Africa.

One of the as yet minimally-researched observations of population migration and emigration is that emigrants seek to replicate the geographical appearance of their homeland in their new country. African cattle-raising populations transmigrated half the continent in search of a similar ecology. White immigrants in Kenya, prior to their expulsion through the so-called Mau Mau uprising (known locally as the Land and Freedom Army), created an English-Scottish landscape in the so-called White Highlands. Most likely the same phenomenon played a role in the establishment of the *mocambos* and *quilombos* in Brazil. Some groups headed for the mountains, not only because there were greater possibilities to stay protected there, but also because they perhaps came from a mountainous area in their African homeland and retained a distant memory of this even two or three generations later. Others recreated a fluvial culture of their African homeland on the banks of Brazilian rivers.[56]

This could be an important aspect of the history of Quartel do Indaiá as well as similar settlements in Minas Gerais. Quite by accident I later discovered similar thoughts to these that I had during my field work in 1979 with Mata Machado Filho (1943, 56), who first visited Quartel do Indaiá in 1935:

> The numerous coconut trees of Indaiá growing in the Quartel did not only serve to give name to the place. It is plausible that the 'quilombolas' were settling there because the place gave them a rare opportunity—judging from the type of homesteads—to reproduce the way of life as in their original (African) homes. The dwellings are covered with palm leaves from those coconut trees which also serve—in various instances—to provide construction material for walls and fences around the open spaces in front of the homesteads.[57]

The most certain reference to the origin of the ancestors of these former *mocambo* or *quilombo* populations are the African language remnants and the "vissungo" work songs. The older people of Quartel do Indaiá were not ones to divulge any information, perhaps as a result of earlier research that was done here. However Sr. Cecilio Assunção Bela Guarda, about 60 years old, offered to accompany a *caixa*, a marching drum (with snare) of Portuguese origin, together with youth from the neighborhood in singing "vissungo" in the Banguëla language.[58] Banguëla (in Bantu transcription *bangela*) vocabulary is primarily comprised of elements which stem from the Umbundu, Kimbundu and, occasionally, other less well-known Angolan languages. A valuable glossary can be found in Aires da Mata Machado Filho's book published in 1943. The word "vissungo," used in the African-Brazilian settlements of Minas Gerais for work-songs, comes from the Umbundu and closely related languages of Central and East Angola, where it simply means "songs." This is a plural form (in Umbundu, *ovisungo*; in Ngangela, *visungo*); the singular in Umbundu is *ocisungo*, and in Ngangela, *cisungo*. It follows from this that the form often used by Brazilian authors, "vissungos," is a double plural.

In addition to the region of S. João da Chapada and Quartel do Indaiá there are numerous other cultural islands in Minas Gerais with African language remnants: amongst others, Milho Verde, where a research program was undertaken by a group of linguists of the Universidade Federal de Juiz de Fora, led by

Professor Zágari and later the German socio-linguist Jürgen Heye, Rio de Janeiro. Jürgen Heye played some of his recordings of "vissungos" from Milho Verde for me in October 1980 in Rio de Janeiro; they were sprinkled with many words from Angolan languages. Mário Roberto Zágari's group, which was working on an *Atlas Linguistico de Minas*, also reported on the continued existence of strange burial rites at Milho Verde:

> A few days before the arrival of the research team at Milho Verde, one of the oldest members of the community had passed away, and the rites preceding the burial were so curious that they attracted the attention of the entire population of Serro and also Diamantina. First they carried the body in a bamboo stretcher covered with a winding sheet. Then they began to drink and sing with fervor. The rites involve all the inhabitants of the village during the entire night. At dawn when everyone is still dizzy, begins the burial procession. Mid-way during their procession, possibly because of exhaustion from the dance and the weight of the corpse to be carried, the walk comes to a halt. Now the second part of the ritual starts. All the people turn round to thrash the dead body with lianas, tree branches, pieces of wood, and the dance starts again, but then without any alcoholic drinks involved. Shortly thereafter, new songs will be intonated. At the end, with everyone covered in sweat and all the alcohol eliminated from the body, the actual funeral procession is initiated. To everyone's surprise, from now on the corpse seems to be lighter, which for them represents the detachment of the spirit from the body.[59]

Only 22 kilometers from Belo Horizonte and about 2 kilometers from the site of the Município de Contágem, the most important industrial complex in Minas Gerais, there is another African-Brazilian community in which the anthropologist Romeu Sabará da Silva from the UFMG and Ms. Cristina de Miranda Mata Machado studied the dance *candombe* (pronounced: *kandombi*). Mumbuca, a more difficult community to penetrate, lies in the Município de Jequitinhonha, in the north of Minas Gerais and about 500 km from Belo Horizonte. In 1973, Mumbuca was a former *quilombo* of about 70 people.[60]

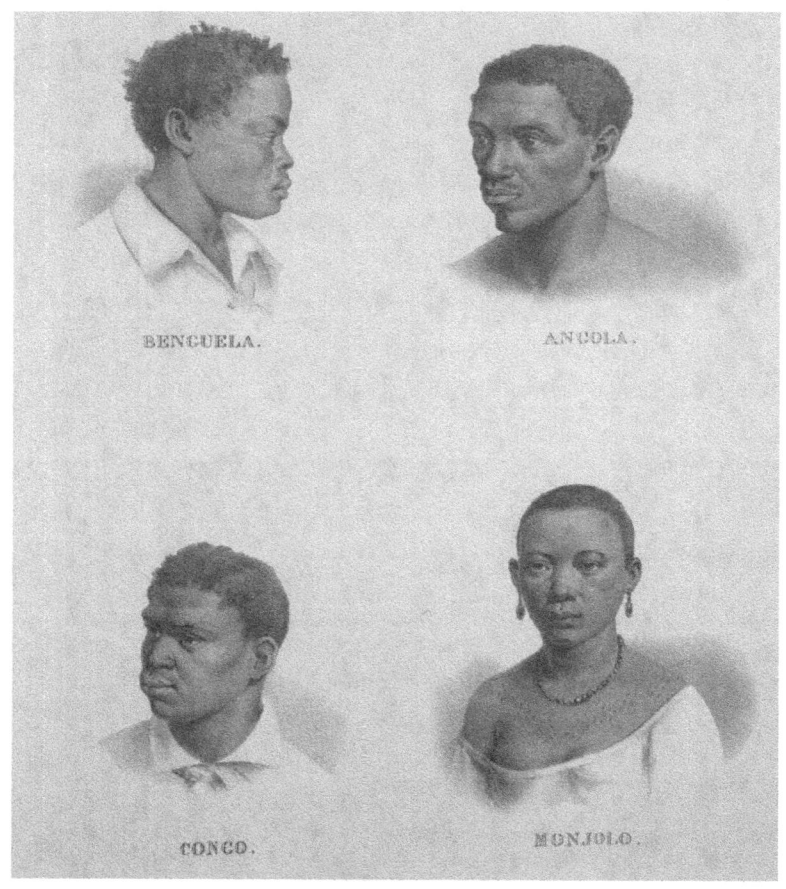

Portraits of members of various "brands" of Africans deported to Brazil, drawn by Johann Moritz Rugendas, 1835. "Benguela" were members of ethnic groups from southwest, Central and East Angola who were shipped out from the Bay of Benguela. "Angola" was predominantly people form the Mbundu Kingdom of Ngola, Ndongo. Reproduced from Johann Moritz Rugendas, 1835.

Detailed rendering of the hairstyles and tattoos of Africans from Bantu-speaking regions by Johann Moritz Rugendas, 1835, in Rio de Janeiro. In this case these were people who most certainly came from northern Mozambique. The elaborate tattoo creations of the Makonde, Makua and other ethnicities in this area at the beginning of the nineteenth century were transferred to the fertile ground of Brazil on which they proliferated in the "laissez-faire" atmosphere of Rio de Janeiro. The tattoo patterns are body-ideograms with many different meanings. Reproduced from Johann Moritz Rugendas, 1835.

Woman selling "acarajé" and other food based on traditional cuisine handed down within the Yorùbá heritage from Salvador/Bahia, 5 October 1975. Photo by G. Kubik (A308).

Street samba in Salvador/Bahia, 5 October 1975. Musicians and dancers perform in the streets of Bomfim, near the beach. A pipe-shaped rattle (chocalho) player showing typical positioning is in the middle. The two other dancers in the foreground concentrate on the complex leg and foot movements they are performing. So-called multiplication techniques in the lower body extremities play a large role in dancing the Brazilian samba. Photo by G. Kubik (A312).

Children in Cafundó making and playing with a boi ("cow"), called ongombe ("cow") in the Cafundó vernacular and created from a green gourd. Bairro de Cafundó, near Salto de Pirapora, the state of São Paulo, Brazil, 1979. Photos by G. Kubik (B 105 and 107).

Central African basket styles in the village of Cafundó: a) dengu type (range: south-central Africa, Angola to Mozambique); b) lisehwa type (East Angola and other Bantu-speaking areas); and c) style found in western Congo (northwest Angola, Democratic Republic of the Congo, Gabon, etc.). Cafundó, May 1979. Photos by G. Kubik (VI/32, 37, 13).

Isolated homestead in the rugged and thickly wooded alpine topography of Minas Gerais. For all intents and purposes, this area was completely inaccessible due to the lack of modern transportation routes. Thanks to a special communication system the residents of the houses scattered throughout the area could contact and warn each other about the approach of tracking expeditions. In the vicinity of Quartel do Indaiá, state of Minas Gerais, May 1979. Photo by G. Kubik (B 212).

In the area of Minas Gerais with remnants of the Banguëla language there are remote homesteads in which the old lifestyle of Angola is still practiced. Here, a woman with a mortar and an upper-weighted pestle, standing in front of a traditional clay dwelling. She is not, however, mashing corn or manioc as would be the case in Angolan villages; she is mashing coffee beans. In the mountainous region near Quartel do Indaiá, state of Minas Gerais, May 1979. Photo by G. Kubik (B 242).

An old sugar cane press near Quartel do Indaiá, state of Minas Gerais, May 1979. Photo by G. Kubik.

Cecilio Assunção Bela Guarda, one of the few people in Quartel do Indaiá who can still sing "vissungos" (visungo) and who still knows some words of the Banguëla tongue, 6 May 1979. Photo by G. Kubik (B 251).

View of the Rio Guaporé, Vila Bela da Santíssima Trindade, Mato Grosso, November 1980. Photos by Moya A. Malamusi.

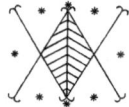

AFRICAN LANGUAGE REMNANTS IN BRAZIL

Language is one of the aspects within a culture's system of communication and expression which is relatively robust in withstanding quick changes. Thus it is an acceptable methodology to look at diachronically (maximum 300 years) wide-ranging language material synchronically within an established scholarly interrogation practice.

It follows that, in the exploration of the cultural African heritage, analysis of the many lexical components of African origin is important. On the one hand, this includes those of autonomous language traditions (e.g. the African language islands in Minas Gerais), and on the other hand, those in the Brazilian language and its various dialects. Modifications which the Portuguese language in Brazil has undergone are for the most part a result of linguistic contacts. These comprise, for example, Spanish in adjacent areas, Amerindian languages, and African languages from Nigeria, Angola and other regions. The modifications include those in a wide range of the lexica, as well as the phonemic (See also Mendonça, 1935). Structural changes which Portuguese underwent in Brazil are not attributable solely to a so-called internal evolution.

When languages split and dialects are formed, we call this the process of divergence. When, however, on the other hand, different languages not stemming from the same parent language become more similar through contact to each other, we call the process convergence. Divergence and convergence are the two basic processes through which languages develop historical relationships to each other. When doing research into processes of convergence, one must also differentiate between two separate procedures by which the process can take place:

1. Complete or partial retention of the mother tongue with borrowings from the foreign language; and

2. Adoption of the foreign language and various degrees of "creolization" through projection of the mother tongue.

In the first case the indigenous language of a specific cultural group is the starting point and the primary reference point for all changes and further developments which take place. The language remains intact as a system even when it undergoes noticeable changes due to borrowings and influences of many different kinds. A striking example in Brazil is the Brazilian language itself in its various forms of dialect. In principal, the descendants of native Portuguese speakers have retained their *own* language.

In the second case the foreign language is the starting point and primary reference point for all changes that take place. In extreme instances a group abandons its language altogether and adopts the foreign tongue, not, however, without projecting major behavior patterns onto it, thus affecting changes. The various forms of Black American English in the United States are a good example. At the far end of the spectrum a complete creolization takes place, as in the Patois in Louisiana, USA. As far as we know there is no example in Brazil of a total creolization of Portuguese by the descendants of speakers of African languages. Suggestions of this kind—for example, that the "secret language" in Cafundó represents a case of creolization—are more sensationalistic and are based on lack of differentiation between the two processes defined above. In the case of Cafundó vocabulary, it is actually *retention* of several convergent languages from Angola which have (in the present) undergone severe shrinking and backfilling of holes with words from the Brazilian language – the colloquial and current mother tongue of Cafundó inhabitants. There is, however, a case of a creole language in Brazil, namely in the "Lanc-Patuá," researched by Julieta de Andrade (1983) and which exists in northern Brazil on the border with French Guiana. Despite the stark phonetic changes *vis-à-vis* the French language and the author's odd orthography, the basis was clearly French.

Both processes will have a simultaneous effect in a situation of cultural contact. Under certain conditions the group will then become *bilingual*. This means that the speakers use both contact languages separately, with a few changes—that is, their own or their mother tongue, and the foreign language—mostly dependent on the situation. For example, they may use the foreign language at official occasions, or at school, and the mother tongue at home. When the two contact languages are closely related, the mother tongue is generally regarded as "dialect" and the foreign language becomes the dominant "high language." This instance occurs often within the spectrum of Portuguese dialects.

In Brazil, as in other parts of the Americas, there is *no* African language still in existence that is a primary communication vehicle. Whatever still exists in the African language islands of Brazil are retentions of partial traditions of African languages, which in a socio-linguistic sense managed to attain a certain autonomy. The users of these language traditions naturally speak Brazilian today as their indigenous tongue. These retentions can still be found in many places in Brazil: the most well-known are the "língua Banguëla" in various communities of African descent in Minas Gerais; the vocabulary of the residents of the villages Cafundó and, until recently, Caxambu near Salto de Pirapora in the state of São Paulo; and the retention of elements from the Yorùbá language in liturgical contexts, specifically the Candomblé religious practices of Bahia. In Bahia and other states, Guilherme dos Santos Barbosa discovered other communities—similar to that of Cafundó—with African language remnants.

The colonial language Portuguese soon established itself as the common language amongst the African population which had been brought to Brazil: firstly, these people lived as dependents of the Luso-Brazilian upper class; and secondly, because the only common language with which members of various African language groups could communicate was the colonists' language. When African populations from neighboring areas in Africa lived together in Brazil, or when ethnically related groups fled from slavery to geographically isolated regions, most of the respective African languages were retained as vehicles of communication. It was only in the twentieth century that they became reduced down to minimal vocabularies.

The influence of African languages on the Brazilian tongue began quite early. Up until the nineteenth century Brazil was a European colony state with an African population majority. The social situation and the concentration of power in the hands of

Portuguese plantation owners and the monarchy, as well as the general defensive psychological mindset of the African population, impeded even regional establishment of any one African language. The cultural grouping division of the Africans had one more result: although Brazil declared its independence on 7 September 1822, it was still governed by the Portuguese House of Braganza; on 1 December 1822 Dom Pedro became the first emperor of the Brazilian kingdom.

His son Pedro II ascended the throne in 1840. Under his rule, the plantation economy, based on coffee, began to develop more and more rapidly from the middle of the nineteenth century. In 1888 his daughter Isabel revoked slavery. A coup followed, organized by outraged plantation owners who felt their economic livelihood threatened, resulting in the end of the monarchy and the declaration of the Brazilian republic in 1889. At this point in time it was much too late for any African languages to establish themselves since the majority of individuals of African ancestry had already accepted Brazilian as their mother tongue. In addition, the African sector of the total population had been declining steadily due to the start of massive European immigration. Soon the Portuguese language was spoken in Brazil by mostly non-Portuguese people, just as it is today in Angola, Mozambique, Guinea-Bissau, Timor, Macau, etc. "Borrowing" took place following certain patterns, all of which can be analyzed once the contact languages have been identified.

Of all the processes involved in the transfer of lexigraphic elements from the African languages, the one with the most important role was the morphemic transfer, in which an expression as well as its meaning is transferred. Very soon, however, changes in meaning (expansions or contractions) took place as shown by the examples of the Angolan words *kilombo, visungo,* etc. Compared to morphemic transfer, semantic transfer, in which foreign morphemes are "translated" (replaced with mother-tongue morphemes), played a relatively small role in the system of African languages. For the standard Brazilian language has been shaped by the Portuguese-origin colonizing culture. Polymorphemic expressions in African languages were absolutely incomprehensible for Brazilians of Portuguese origin, who had no portal to either structural or conceptual understanding of their enslaved laborers' languages. Analogous processes like, for example the direct translation from the French "gratte-ciel" into the English "skyscraper," were rarely possible for the Luso-Brazilians.

In the phonemic area, too, African languages influenced the Brazilian. Numerous phonetic differences between some of Brazilian's dialect variations and Portuguese can be traced back to African language influences, in which the Angolan languages had a noticeable impact. The conflict of Yorùbá with Portuguese in Bahia thus may have been less extreme—due to several coincidental phonetic commonalities between the two languages, e.g. the large number of vocal phoneme, the nasalized vowels, etc.—than the one of the Bantu languages.

Influences also took place in the opposite direction. The phonemics of the Portuguese language influenced the pronunciation of borrowed words transferred into Brazilian. Even the autonomous African language traditions in Brazil were affected by these Portuguese phonemics. In the first case, this often took place through the written characters. By this I mean that pronunciation of borrowings from African languages, when transcribed using Portuguese orthography, became aligned retroactively over time with Portuguese phonemic elements. In the second case, that is, in bilingual African-Brazilian communities which still supported African vocabulary, a similar adaptation took place in a completely verbal process. An example is the present state of the "African language" of the village of Cafundó in the state of São Paulo. Its vocabulary, with roots in Angolan languages, can be identified as such, but still has undergone some changes in pronunciation due to the influence of regional Brazilian as it is spoken around Salto de Pirapora.[61]

The Brazilian vocabulary of African borrowings contains to a great extent elements from Umbundu, Kimbundu, Yorùbá and Kikoongo. In addition, elements from other African languages occasionally come to the fore, an example is the word *cachaça* (distilled alcohol, "sugar cane schnapps"), which in the opinion of my colleague Donald Kachamba, comes from the Chicheŵa/Cinyanja word for the same product, *kachasu*. Chichewa is spoken in Malawi, East Zambia and parts of northern Mozambique. The same word is also known in some neighboring languages around Mozambique. In these regions, however, alcohol is not brewed from sugar cane, as in Brazil, but from corn and manioc. Various sources confirm that many members of the Maravi group (from today's Malawi and north Mozambique) in particular were amongst those taken after 1815 to Brazil (Carreira 1979; Debret 1834; Koelle 1854; Rugendas 1835).

Which African languages dominated in Brazil during the epoch of slavery? An answer to this question can be found in contemporary relationships in the areas where Africans originated, since the process of lingual transformations began not on Brazilian soil, but actually took place in Africa.

In those regions of Africa that were directly affected by transatlantic slaving, a unique economic model was developing along the caravan and trade routes. This new economy was dependent on from coastal commerce and the regular appearance of trade caravans.

The framework of these contacts led to specific culture-altering factors along the Central African transport routes, often to the extent that a specific "trade route culture" formed. Research into the indigenous languages in these zones in which widely used languages proliferated (Hausa, Yorùbá in West Africa; Kimbundu, Umbundu, etc. in Angola; Kiswahili in East Africa) confirms the use of countless words borrowed from the common language or the European language of the slave traders on the coast. Most of the enslaved peoples from inner Africa sold to middle men learned the common language of the region as they journeyed to the coast, a journey which could take many weeks. The enslaved Africans would begin to talk with each other in the regional trade language, using their mother tongue only when communicating with those of their own cultural group. This explains, in the examination of collective African vocabulary, the predominance of words stemming from African trade languages (like Umbundu, Kimbundu in Angola) or languages of countries with higher population density (like Yorùbá). These were the languages which established themselves. If this is not taken into account, the fragmentation of a linguistic finding in Brazil can result in an inaccurate picture of the true origin of enslaved Africans and their ethnicity. To a great extent it was members of smaller and less well-armed ethnicities who were sold into slavery. Their indigenous languages had no chance—with the exception of a few words (important reference terms)—of flourishing in the Americas. The language that did continue to exist in Brazil was the common tongue of the respective African region. Thus, the high proportion of Umbundu words in the African linguistic sampling of Brazil (such as from Minas Gerais, or in the vocabulary of the community of Cafundó as investigated by dos Santos Barbosa and me) does not mean that the ancestors of these communities were Ovimbundu. Rather, it means that they were abducted from areas in which Umbundu functioned as a trade language.

An investigation of African language remnants in Brazil therefore requires a new methodological orientation, in light of recent linguistic and socio-linguistic research in Africa. Particularly in the area of the much ramified Bantu languages, earlier studies in Brazil often proceeded from insufficient, even faulty assessments:

1. The "African words" of Brazilian interviewees were written down in the form of single lexigraphic items out of context.

2. Phonemic analyses were not carried out prior to transcription.

3. No significance was ascribed to tonal elements.

4. The words were transcribed by ear, usually in an orthography based on Portuguese phonemics. Occasionally some odd spellings crop up, as in an article published in 1980 in Spanish by the group Carlos Vogt, Peter Fry and Maurizio Gnerre from the Universidade de Campinas on the "secret languages" of Cafundó (*las lenguas secretas de Cafundó*). In this essay the authors employ an orthography similar to the one used by nineteenth-century European travelers in Central Angola (such as Henrique A. Dias de Carvalho, 1890), including diacritical marks that are completely unnecessary in the Bantu languages, for example, "kwēda pra kõžēga karũga" (Vogt 1980, 28). Absolutely unproblematic Bantu words from Cafundó like *mukanda* (piece of writing, book), *mafumbura*, (illness caused by external factors) or *ngombi* (cattle) are transcribed as "mukãda," "mafũbura"

and "ngõbi."

5. The "identification" of the collected lexigraphic elements was usually attempted in Brazil with the help of any lexicons at hand or through written correspondence with African language scholars at other universities (e.g. in Europe or South Africa) who were sent word lists of the baffling items.

When one of these words happened to appear in a dictionary of Kikoongo, it seemed to confirm that remnants of the Kikoongo language lived on in the African-Brazilian community. However, the presence of single words in a random African language for which a dictionary happens to be available, and separated from an African-Brazilian context, is certainly not conclusive proof. It is a dubious undertaking in terms of methodology to try and reconstruct historical connections this way. In all probability the same word that our researcher finds in a Kikoongo lexicon exists not only in Kikoongo, but also in a whole cluster of other interrelated languages of the central-west African area. To put this into perspective, consider words that have such a wide interregional diffusion in Africa that they are almost universal. Such a word, for example, is *kulima* (to work in the fields). It belongs to the Bantu languages all the way from the Atlantic coast of Angola (Umbundu, Kimbundu, Ngangela, etc.) into southern Central Africa (Chichewa) over to the Indian Ocean (Kiswahili, etc.).

One criterion for establishing an historical relationship between lexical elements from any African diaspora area and African areas must be a morphological *and* semantic identity. One aspect of these two is not sufficient to prove linguistic relationships in the distant past. In those places where an identity can no longer be confirmed due to changes in meaning or pronunciation of a word, but rather only a similarity is observed, it may be possible to reconstruct how the respective mutation on one side or the other of the Atlantic Ocean came about.

Attempts to compare African-Brazilian elements with those in African languages on the basis of *written notation*—in which the speech tones are rarely noted—must be undertaken with extreme care. In order to do this, the African-Brazilian elements must first be transcribed into the orthography of the respective African languages from which they presumably originate. A small handbook published by the Instituto Nacional de Línguas in Luanda (1980) is available for Angolan languages and their orthographies, in which a modern orthography for no fewer than six languages (Kikoongo, Kimbundu, Umbundu, Cokwe, Mbunda and Nyaneka) has been established based on phonemic analyses.[62]

Most of the African elements in Brazil have been recorded in Brazilian literature with Portuguese spelling, which leads to serious problems. A word like *nyamanyara* (young girl) from Cafundó vernacular would be written in this spelling as "nhamanhara": the Portuguese o-endings always raise doubts in such notations whether the respective ending is a [ɔ], [o] or [u]. For example, is "calumbo" *kalumbo* or *kalumbu*? Despite this, it is possible to transfer the words appearing in various writings at a later time into a Bantu orthography, providing a basis for comparison. In this way, for example, Banguëla language elements of Angolan origin collected by Aires da Mata Machado Filho (1943, 122-38) in São João da Chapada, Minas Gerais, could be re-written as follows: "cuata" as *kwata* (grasp, catch), "curima" as *kulima* (to work in the fields), "ochito" as *oxitu* (meat), "quimbundo" as *Kimbundu* (member of the Kimbundu ethnic group; in Minas Gerais, generally, African), "sengue" as *senge* (woods, forest), "uanda" as *wanda* (fishing net), and "vissungo" as *visungo* (songs).

Researching the West African portion of African-Brazilian vocabulary is somewhat less easy. Tracing Yorùbá words in Bahia also relies on a transcription into Yorùbá—for simple cases like Oxum is *Ọṣun* and Xangô is *Ṣàngó*—all the way through to complicated ones. However, one of the problems here is that not only are the Portuguese transcriptions of Yorùbá words poorly rendered, but unfortunately so is the missionary-influenced Yorùbá orthography that is officially recognized in Nigeria, with its diacritical marks (such as dots under the vowels to distinguish an open ọ and ẹ from closed ones), as well as the replication of nasalized vowels by adding an -n. Examples of this include *ẹrin* (elephant), *ọba* (king), *ọrun* (heaven), *ẹrin* (laughing), and *ọlọrun* (owner of the heavens, one manifestation of "God"). Thus, the characters of Yorùbá, Fon and Ewe words (this last one having an excellent orthography thanks to Dietrich Westermann) are not directly comparable.

It is preferable to commit phrases or other spoken elements from Brazil to a tape recording that is then compared to corresponding material in Africa by playing the Brazilian recordings to African subjects and asking for their commentary. I did this type of research in January 1981 in Luanda, Angola with speech- and word-samplings from the community of Bairro de Cafundó which I had made in April 1979.

The African vocabulary recalled by the residents of Cafundó in the area of Salto de Pirapora, about 140 kilometers from São Paulo, represents one of the most interesting cases of African language remnants in Brazil. A similar vocabulary was used in the three other now-dissolved communities of Angolan descendants in the same region. The identity of the "language" of Cafundó with that of the village of Caxambu, a few kilometers away, was confirmed in a long interview which Guilherme dos Santos Barbosa and I had with Sr. Emiliano Jovino de Almeida, about 65 years old, the former village leader of the community of Caxambu.[63] My 1979 research in Cafundó and the subsequent checking of word samples with Angolan interlocutors in Zambia and Angola (June to September 1979), as well as a control-group discussion with Dr. Kazadi wa Mukuna from the Democratic Republic of Congo, revealed that Cafundó words all originated in Angola and directly neighboring regions. With the exception of one single word from the Tupi (an Amerindian language)—the word "tupã" for the Supreme Being—no lexical items from other languages, above all not from West Africa, can be identified.

Occasionally a change or expansion of meaning has taken place in the Cafundó words vis-à-vis their Angolan counterparts. For example in the Cafundó vocabulary *masangu* means rice (in Angola, millet); *kulima* means not only to work in the fields, but "to work" in general. Dr. Kazadi wa Mukuna points to this as it also exists in Congo-Kiswahili. The change of meaning which the word *jambi* has undergone is strange: while in the west-central African languages different variations of this word (e.g. *nzambi* in Kikoongo and Kimbundu, and *njambi* in Ngangela, *zambi* in Cokwe, etc.) are translated as "God," "Highest Being,' in Cafundó it means "a nossa Senhora" (the Holy Mother Mary)!

In the "língua Africana" of Cafundó, as village leader Otavio

Caetano calls the vocabulary, rules from the Bantu grammar are no longer evident, neither conjugations nor even a reminder of the former noun classes and their grammatical agreement. The vocabulary comprises isolated lexigraphic elements—nouns, verbs, adjectives, but no prepositions. Verbs appear either in the infinitive (for example, *konoa* or *konowa*, "to drink") or in another form which was retained in place of the infinitive (*varya* or *valya*, "to eat," instead of *kulya*). In the phonetic area, changes also occurred respective to the original languages, like *andalu* (fire) in the Cafundó vocabulary compared to *ondalu* in Umbundu. In addition, the pronunciation of Bantu words was adapted to align with the phonology of the so-called Caipira dialect of Portuguese spoken in the state of São Paulo (cf. Amaral 1976).

The Cafundó vocabulary of around 200 to 300 words must have reached its final form during a period when most of the Umbundu-, Kimbundu- and Kikoongo-speakers amongst the ancestors had died. Vocabulary was lost from one generation to the next, and there was likely already a very rapid loss of grammar in the first generation of Brazil-born enslaved Africans. Thereby it appears that many ancestors of Cafundó families arrived only during the final phase of transatlantic slaving, somewhere from the middle of the nineteenth century.

Dona Benedita Pires Pedroso, born in 1907 (according to Cartório de Registro Civil, Nascimento N. 244, Município de Salto de Pirapora), to whom we are exceedingly grateful for her repeated hospitality, told us that, as a boy of about twelve, her grandfather was "stolen" (*roubado*) in the Congo (probably modern-day North Angola).

Dona Benedita could still sing a song with Kikoongo words that she had learned from her grandfather.[64] Members of the oldest generation today in Cafundó, those who were born after the turn of the century, often are only the third post-slave abduction generation. If we count back 25 to 30 years per generation, Dona Benedita's grandfather would have been born between 1847 and 1857 in the Congo. Unfortunately she could not recall her grandfather's African name. She told us that he was usually called "Congo."

Today the vocabulary of Cafundó is used in playful conversations when outside visitors come. In Appendix (A) there is a transcription of a tape-recorded conversation illustrating this. In those spots where African words are missing, new constructions are invented, Portuguese prepositions are inserted, and new concepts are created from available vocabulary. For instance, the Umbundu word for "moon" (*osai*) has long since been forgotten. To compensate for this void, they created the form *kumbi d'oteke* (literally, the sun of night). Lightning is *andalu d'ovava* (the fire of the water); in the inversion *ovava d'andalu* (the water of the fire) this construction means petroleum (for domestic lamps). Kambelela means "meat"; "fish" is *kambelela d'ovava* (literally, the meat of the water).

In particular, the village leader Otavio Caetano appears to be very creative in this respect. One can assume that some of these constructions were generated only in response to many questions from visitors, including the linguistic teams of the Universidade de Campinas beginning in May 1978 upon the "discovery" of Cafundó.[65] Many visitors asked questions by way of this format: "How do you say 'hello' in 'African'?"[66] The residents of former slave settlements try to their best ability to please their interviewers. The main interviewee, Otavio Caetano, tried to "reconstruct" the language which, due to shrinkage, had reached its possibly lowest-ever volume around 1977. Some of the constructions quoted above are typical products of efforts to revive the language. The residents of Cafundó are suddenly becoming interested again in the language of their ancestors.

Following my last visit in November 1980 I received a strange letter from Abdenico Pires, about 30 years old, a nephew of Dona Benedita Pires Pedroso and son of Silvino Pires. He wrote the following in this letter of 20 January 1981: "...Mas se posso fazer pergunta então, por favor, Mestre Kubik, como devo fazer para receber dictionário Africano e Português? Palavras portuguêsas que eu quero saber em Africano" (But if I can make an inquiry then, please, Professor Kubik, what should I do to receive an African and Portuguese dictionary? [Below are] Portuguese words that I want to know in African):[67]

| *praia* | *promissoria* | *escrever* | *prefeito* |
| *mangue* | *protesto* | *ler* | *vereador* |

mar	pais	primário	candidato
morro	estado	ginazio	ciência
casar	município	colegio	istoria
construir	território	faculdade	rodovia
viajar	capital	eleição	avenida
comprar	bairro	voto	rua
vender	vila	politica	centro
lucro	património	partido	juiz
prejuizo	interior	govemo	policia
violão	litoral	deputado	detetive
sanfona	campos	senador	profição
contrato	mata	ministro	educação
civilização			

Nothing could have more clearly expressed the wishes of the young generation of Cafundó families than this unintentional "semantic differential" which Abdenico presented in his letter. It is striking that a large number of the words are from the areas of politics, society and education. Abdenico is looking for words in "African" (in Cafundó one believes that there is one uniform African language) that would express those ideas and concepts most important to him in the language of his ancestors. Of particular significance in the sought-after vocabulary are words of "advancement" and "progress," although the list does start, rather characteristically, with words associated with the past: praia (beach), mangue (mango), mar (the ocean), moro (hill); and continues with verbs like casar (to marry), construir (to build a house), viajar (to travel), comprar (to buy), vender (to sell). Then words like "prejudice," "protest," "escrever" (to write) and "ler" (to read) appear, and finally there is a number of political-educational terms, and the list ends with the word civilization.

From "praia" (beach) to civilization, is not this something like a self-representation of the African in Brazil, documented in keywords and memory tags? The way that African-Brazilians see themselves retrospectively today? Abdendico's words, which he wants to know in "African," are nothing more than a chronological visual novel of the history of the African people in Brazil—from the very first impression following the crossing in steerage, of the beach (!) all the way through to the aspired-after "civilization," a concept modeled on that of the one-time oppressors, but then translated back into an African idea so as to signal political independence.

There is nothing to be found about such concepts in the documentation about Cafundó. After the discovery of this community, as a result of a criminal case in 1978, a wave of mystification about the place and its residents spread through the media, notably in reference to the "African dialect." The mere combination of the words in titles of everyday newspaper articles speaks for itself: "Os mistérios de um dialeto negro – Unicamp começa a pesquisa no local" (*O Estado de S. Paulo*, 2 May 1978); "Nova comunidade negra descoberta em Minas Gerais" (*O Estado de S. Paulo*, 14 May 1978); "Os negros perdidos do Cafundó" (*Foìhetim*, 14 May 1978); and "Cafundó, um mistério para os antropólogos" (*O the state of São Paulo*, 22 April 1979).

That is how this tiny African-Brazilian community looked from a Luso-Brazilian perspective – and not only in the mass media. The pattern is similar to that in colonial and neo-colonial popular literature about Africa. It speaks of the residents of Cafundó as *negros perdidos* ("lost black people"), who do not speak a language, just a "Negro dialect" (*dialeto negro*). The place itself is full of "secrets, mysteries" (*mistérios*). In Brazil new back commulnities are always "discovered" (*nova comunidade negra descoberta...*) and in Cafundó a "secret language" with a "ritual function" is still spoken (cf. Carlos Vogt et al. 1980).

My associates also expressed their reactions to Cafundó following our visit together there in October 1980. In their eyes, Cafundó is simply an African village transplanted to Brazil, in which one lives like back in the homeland. My colleagues saw absolutely nothing "mysterious" in it. They simply found industrious, hospitable people who wanted to hold on to some of their cultural heritage. The poor condition of the teeth of many residents, however, surprised my African colleagues: young people were already missing their front teeth, which also hindered their speech. It seems that these teeth are removed on purpose. It is a custom that we are familiar with from Angola, and one which links the residents of Cafundó in yet another way with their ancestors. Neither my African colleagues nor I were able to elicit an explanation for this custom from anyone. However, there is a reference that has been handed down orally from the Umbundu Angolans as follows: "The missing front teeth are deliberately extracted to leave a door open for the spirit (or the soul) to leave the human at night-time."[68]

On the first day of our visit a quite exciting attempt was made to establish verbal contact between my African colleagues and the people in the house of the village leader Otavio Caetano. Using the "universal" Bantu dictionary, we identified the first link: those forms with regular phonetic and meaning analogies throughout the contemporary Bantu languages. This time Otavio Caetano was not the interviewee, rather, the leader showed great interest in questioning my African colleagues. Since they knew only a little Portuguese, one of them, Moya, had learned some of the Cafundó vocabulary in just one week's time and so was able to communicate with that. The other, Donald Kachamba, discovered a music-making partner in the boy "Jovenio" (*juvenil*). "Jovenio" played the accordion, Donald Kachamba the guitar. This was the only place in Brazil that this African musician and composer played together with anyone of his own volition.

Regarding conversations in the Cafundó vocabulary which I had tape-recorded, Moya said, "I don't think they are talking about anything in particular. They know these words and are just *building up*."[69] The tonality of the Cafundó vocabulary elicited astonishment and even some derisive comments on the part of my colleagues.[70] As for me, the diction and tonality, especially of Otavio Caetano, were reminiscent of the manner in which "Bantu" was spoken in some 1930s adventure movies (like Tarzan). The tonality of the Cafundó conversation is apparently influenced by the manner in which the Luso-Brazilian world imagines that a "preto" (black person) speaks "African." Regarded thus through sociolinguistic eyes, the Cafundó vocabulary is not just an African language tradition that found a continuation in Brazil, but also almost like a colonial-neurotic manifestation of the transference of former slaveholders' ideas about the character of their slaves' "African dialect" to their modern-day counterparts.

There are reflections of the past in the Cafundó vocabulary for "homen preto" (black person) and "homen blanco" (white person). Cafundó residents regard themselves and all people of African descent as "vimbundo," whereby it must be said that this ethnic nomenclature for a group in Angola, the Ovimbundu (sing. Ocimbundu) has undergone a broadening of meaning over time. It may be that the identification of those sold into slavery with their first (black) slave holders and oppressors, combined with a wider-scoped learning of the Umbundu trade language, played a role in this. Use of the term *kafombe* for a white person is baffling. The origin of this word was puzzling to me for a long time, since there was no such word to be found in any Angolan language known to me. The Angola/Congo names for the "white person" are *mundele, ocindele, cindele,* etc. in the various languages. Only during my recent visit to Angola in January 1981 did a possible solution come to the fore. M. Eduardo Dias de Figueiredo from Luanda suggested the following explanation: *kafombe* is a corruption of the Kimbundu word *kifumbe* (criminal, bandit). Our subject literally wrote, "*kafombe* – corruptela de *kifumbe* (pl. *ifumbe*) que significa violador, bandido e pode também ser aplicado aos brancos Europeus que no passado agarravam as pessoas para a escravidão e posteriormente para o contrato" (*kafombe* – a corruption of *kifumbe* (pl. *ifumbe*) which means violator, crook and can also be applied to white Europeans that in the past seized the people for slavery and later for contract [laboring]).[71] Manuel António Sebastião from the Departamento Nacional de Museus e Monumentos also made similar remarks independently of M. Eduardo Dias de Figueredo in a conversation with me a few days earlier in Luanda. Thus it is possible that the term *kafombe* comes from Kimbundu or one of its related Angolan languages, and that in Brazilian groups around Salto de Pirapora who were impacted by the misdeeds of the slave traders, the concept of "criminal" and "bandit" was applied generally to white Europeans. Considering that the so-called "bandeirantes" comprised a large number of adventurers and criminals, this would have been a logical process and simultaneously a documentation of a critical position taken up by the enslaved vis-à-vis their oppressors.

In 1981 I took a recording of a conversation in Cafundó between village leader Otavio Caetano and a relative, Maria de Lourdes in Angola.[72] In the presence of numerous guests from various regions, I played the recording in the house of musician Kituxi in Luanda on Janurary 1, 1981, asking for comments. It elicited startling results. Arnoldo Sebastião Vicente Junior, who came from southern Angola, said that the recordings are closest to the language as one speaks it in Huíla (Wila) province, south of the Bay of Benguela. He knew most of the words. "Andalu" (fire) corresponds to *ndalu* (which has the same meaning) in the Umbundu language of Huambo, Benguela and Lobito. However what was most noticeable for him was, in particular, the tone in the Cafundó pronunciation, one which points to southern Angola, actually into the Kwanyama-speaking region, he said. For example, in the interview Otavio Caetano says at one point *kupopyá* (to speak) with the rising tone on the final vowel, characteristic for the southern pronunciation of Umbundu. Other phrases, for example, *ombambi vavuro* (much coldness), originated in the Kimbundu language from northwest Angola; written correctly, it would be *mbambi yavulu*. It must be noted, however, that the word appears as *ombambi*—with the same meaning—in Umbundu as well. *Ovava* (water), in contrast, is in any case Umbundu, since water is called *menya* in Kimbundu.[73]

One of the few Cafundó vocabulary words whose origin I had never been able to identify was *kamanako*, translated by residents as "criança" (child). M. Eduardo Dias de Figueiredo in Luanda assured me that a word with this phonology and meaning exists in Songo. This seems to me to be historically significant. It is known that the Songo, an ethnic group in the Angolan hinterland, were severely affected by transatlantic slaving. However, relatively little ethnographical material about the Songo exists. The only person who worked extensively in this area was the Austrian ethnologist Dr. Karl Höfer who died in 1975 in Luanda. In collaboration with an Angolan assistant from the Songo region, over the course of several years, he compiled a Songo-Portuguese dictionary during his work at the Instituto de Investigacão Cientifica de Angola, Luanda. He showed me this dictionary in Vienna in 1975 a few weeks before his death. He also had a large collection of slides from his field research with the Songo. His life's work is now housed at the Instituto de Antropologia, University of Coimbra, Portugal.

The presence of even just one Songo expression in the Cafundó vocabulary can be ascribed a greater significance since it gives a clue to the ethnic constitution of the ancestry of the Salto de Pirapora enslaved population. As I have mentioned above, the proportional relationship of the share of various African languages in an African-Brazilian sample (like that of Cafundó) does not reflect the proportional relationship of ethnicities of the abducted people. These ratios usually deviate considerably, for as a rule it was either the language of the majority, or the trade language of the respective African region that established itself in Brazil. Thanks to one or the other word in Songo, Lunda, Luvale, etc. as well as observations of the Angolan interviewees (above) regarding tonality, we can put our finger on some of the actual regions of origin.

A question that is asked again and again in connection with African language remnants in Brazil is, why they are even still in use today? Why did their use not stagnate completely? Dos Santos Barbosa accounts for the continued existence of the Cafundó vocabulary due to the particular socio-political situation of its residents since the time of slavery when they lived as prisoners, constantly under surveillance and subjected to rigid control. To a certain extent, Cafundó residents' consciousness of their ancestors' condition has been internalized over and over again in every new generation up through today. This has become a sort of life-view in relation to the residents of the surrounding area, to the "fazendeiros" and to the administration in Salto de Pirapora.

It was necessary for enslaved Africans and their descendants to communicate amongst each other without being understood by members of the property-owners' social class. This explains why the "African language" continued to exist for a relatively long time following the formal emancipation of enslaved Africans in 1888. The most important point mentioned by dos Santos Barbosa, who has been studying the Cafundó community since May 1978, is that residents don't speak their "African language" at all when they are amongst themselves. He writes:

> Since the 'language of Cafundó' is a fragmented representation of a living cultural heritage, left behind by the ancestors, we should understand that (1) those captives were living under intense individual and group pressure, (2) that they were living under constant surveillance, so that they should not communicate with each other or attempt to flee, (3) that they were living under rigid control to produce as much as they were able. Under such circumstances, it is natural that they would take recourse to a defense reaction, developing a way of communicating between themselves without any risk of being understood by outsiders.
>
> This was possible because of the language they had inherited, which became an instrument of defense in the presence of the oppressor. When the oppressor was absent, there was no need for using it.
>
> Today, the Cafundó language is something like a game of words without any nexus, even occasionally incorporating elements from Tupi-Guarani, an Amerindian language, e.g. the word *tupã*, and the constant interpolation of Portuguese words in the conversations, e.g. *mas, tá, sempre, ah*, etc. This means that the (African) language was losing lexemes for lack of usage. The people of Cafundó, like those of Caxambu, do not speak 'the African language' when they are among themselves; there is no need for it. The matter is similar to what it was like during the days of slavery; with the oppressor absent, the defense is dismantled. Today, the TV, the newspapers, the radio, the tape-recorders and we represent the figure of the oppressor! So many times have I heard them talk in their 'dialect,' so that I could not understand.[74]

The African language remnants and likewise many other Africanisms were a barrier, a dam, against a complete cultural depersonalization for the African cultural island communities of Brazil. The reason why African language remnants exist in Cafundó and other communities, such as in Minas Gerais, may be inferred from the following historical development. For those coming from a cohesive cultural area, for example from Angola, a basis for verbal communication developed quickly amongst newly-arrived enslaved Africans. Either one language established itself, or elements from several related languages merged. An *African code* of the affected slave communities developed which allowed residents of the *senzalas* on the plantations to communicate quickly and confidentially with each other, and at the same time serve as an expression of their solidarity as prisoners in the face of their oppressors. The enslaved Africans lived on two psychological levels. Officially, they adopted the language of the slaveholders, and after a short time spoke it in their own homes and settlement communities—an expression of the progressive identification of the oppressed with the oppressor and his values. At the same time, however, indigenous language and cultural values, inaccessible to the oppressor, continued to exist as expression of a simultaneous resistance to the oppressor. Thanks to the possibility of communicating in a code indecipherable by the plantation owners, the African community enjoyed the advantage of being able to rapidly reach confidential agreements and make decisions, if need be even in the presence of "fazendeiros" family members.

Conversations in African remnant languages were not necessarily directed *against* the strangers who were present. Just as in every subculture, the code served to express sanctioned information that was to be concealed from oppressors with dissimilar values. The words for genitals have been preserved in the Cafundó vocabulary, as has an expression for sexual intercourse, *nyepa*. The Cafundó expression for "vagina," *matako*, is interesting, because in most of the Angolan languages, and also in Kikoongo, *matako* means "buttocks," or, as in Umbundu, *omatako* means simply "naked."[75] Only in Luanda does it refer to the female sexual organ: *mataku* (sing. *itaku*) there means labia majora. Other words which generally are not shared with visitors to Cafundó have been passed down, for example *kaxapitu* (flatulence, breaking wind). Thus, an important function of the Cafundó vocabulary was to preserve a sort of psychological space, an own identity, so as to resist a cultural absorption. Just as with the behavioral patterns we know of colonized peoples in Africa, as a comparison the Cafundó vocabulary had a two-pronged socio-psychological function. On the one hand it was resistance in the face of claims of superiority by the surrounding non-African culture. On the other hand, in an internalization process of foreign expectations (recognized in the psychology of colonization), inhabitants began to align precisely with the stereotype of a "negro dialect" as the Luso-Brazilians of the ruling classes saw it: vocabulary poverty, no grammar, very few abstract concepts, silly-sounding "houseboy" style of speaking with many "úmbáà," exactly like the "Negroes" portrayed in Tarzan films and African adventure novels of the 1930s.

Over time the African code receded due to its situational context, as the social condition of the residents was changing, as well as the increasing temporal distance from their African ancestors. Structural characteristics of the Bantu languages were forgotten and the lacunae in the vocabulary which soon appeared were filled with Portuguese conjunctions, prepositions, etc.

Our main interlocutors in reference to Cafundó vocabulary. The leader of the village Otavio Caetano (left) at a performance of a "Samba de Cafundó," together with Noel Rosa de Almeida (right), who plays the bumbu (from the Portuguese "bombo") drum. Bairro de Cafundó near Salto de Pirapora, state of São Paulo, April 1979. Photo by G. Kubik (B 142).

One of the eldest Cafundó residents, Silvino Pires, about 70, winnowing rice. He carries out this task rhythmically and with click sounds and other verbal accompaniment. Bairro de Cafundó near Salto de Pirapora, state of São Paulo, April 1979. Photo by G. Kubik (B 135).

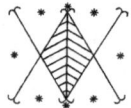

DANCE DRAMAS, POPULAR THEATER AND FIGHTING GAMES

Apart from the linguistic realm there are many other communicative and expressive African-Brazilian manifestations which owe their existence and further development on Brazilian soil to their function as symbols of cultural resistance and cultural identity retention. During Brazilian colonial times (aside from any individual freedom declarations and escape of isolated African population segments to so-called *quilombos*) there was no extensive revolution or national overthrow/change of government as happened in 1798 in Haiti. However, over the centuries there was a certain constant, latent disposition to revolution. The white population, which was still a minority into the nineteenth century, sensed this and was afraid of this potential, as can be inferred, for example, from the following report by Rugendas (1835, 23):

> The imbalance in some parts of America between material power and [population] numbers is enormous, as these data show. It is not simple to explain how it can be possible that so many black people can be held in such a situation of obedience and slavery by so few whites; even when one does not take into account the advantages of the whites: their stable positions – in short their estate of legal power and their possessions, and also the potential support from Europe in the event of a Negro uprising. For experience has shown that in such an actual case pure force would be decisive, and then the color black would prevail in most colonies.... The ultimate emancipation of Negro slaves in America may or may not be their natural right; it may or may not impinge on the legal rights of the owners; in any case it is an unavoidable

natural consequence of the effect of once-existing powers, and the owners can only preserve their own legal rights by voluntarily surrendering.

The preservation of African languages as an internal group communication vehicle was a guarantee of effective communication in a moment of crisis. Functioning in a similar way, knowledge of speech passages in connection with musical instruments (like drums) was retained for a long time. It continues to be passed down today in the form of verbal or syllabic patterns integrated with drum passages.[76]

In respect to preservation of the African "nations" groups and their modern-day transformation into cultural groups on Brazilian soil, numerous so-called *folguedos*, as Rossini Tavares de Lima identified them, served an important function. Folguedo is a type of historical dance drama or popular theater/dance theater characterized by a dramatic performance associated with a parade and a glimpse back to episodes and events of the distant past, which are ceremoniously presented. One can read an extensive description of *folguedos* by Tavares de Lima (1962). They presented manifestations such as "Maracatú," "Mozambique," "Bumba-meu-Boi," "Congada" and many more. Several of them are shown as outdoor theater in which elements of ancestors' political structures from the African homeland are handed down. The conveyers of these traditions are association groups with established members.

African parallels to these Brazilian dance drama associations can be found in many areas of predominantly Bantu-speaking Africa, and especially in those where a similar socio-cultural situation (but without historical connection to the Brazilian events) during the epoch of colonialism led to comparable compensating reactions. An example is the *mganda* associations near Lake Malawi (in Malawi, Zambia, Tanzania and Mozambique), where military order and discipline as experienced during World War I are passed down in the framework of a dance drama with a parade dance and a "dance in place."[77] There the performers, as in the Brazilian *folguedos*, are categorized hierarchically by class with a king, a queen and various character figures playing socio-political roles. The various groups often participate against each other in public competitions. Similarly organized associations of women, known as *chiwoda* and *visekese* have been formed in emulation of the men's associations. Dance drama associations that one could define with the Brazilian expression *folguedo* are also known from Angola.[78]

Based on recent research findings, one can re-examine the Brazilian *folguedos* using Bantu-African drama associations, which are similar in both structure and organization. Without a doubt, all Brazilian *folguedos* originated in Brazil. Their content does not derive directly from African *folguedos*, but there is certainly a discernible African heritage evident in their structure, their organization, the strongly marked kinetic repertoire and many other areas.

Researching Brazilian *folguedos* also necessitates a methodological reorientation. It is important to differentiate between "deep structure" and "surface structure." Above all, the researcher must separate distinct content and material from underlying meanings, all the while factoring in other areas of expression and behavior. When, for example, a *folguedo* like the Marujada depicts a Portuguese ship voyage across the Atlantic, with Portuguese kings and captains, it follows that this *folguedo* is just as little a continuation of Portuguese folklore on Brazilian soil as Giuseppe Verdi's "Aida" is one of Egyptian folklore. Marujada is a dominant Bantu-African tradition in Bahia. However, this does not imply that the Marujada can be directly traced back to any particular Angolan or other Bantu-African *folguedo*. Stylistically it is a Bantu-African extension. And one can only unearth this by scratching beneath the surface structure and looking at the motion structure of the entire work, such as the kinetic choreography of the sword dance, or the entrance of the wooden percussive instruments, or the way the actors move during the sung dialogues, or the harmonies and antiphonal structures of the songs. There is hardly a trace of Portugal in this. As Olly Wilson set out in his presentation as a member of the panel "African Roots of Music in the Americas" (Chairman: Gerard Behague) at the 12th Congress of the International Musicological Society in Berkeley, 21-27 August 1977, Africa's most significant contribution to African diaspora cultures up to now is in the kinetic-motion area. In this respect, the Brazilian *folguedos* have hardly been investigated at all. What has been mentioned here about the Marujada is also applicable to Capoeira, Maculelê and other presentations.

Amongst south Brazilian population segments with roots in the Congo region who were originally speakers of Kikoongo, aspects of the political organization of the former Kingdom of Kôngo have been preserved up to today in one of the most important African-Brazilian dance dramas, the "Congada" or "Festa do Congo." It climaxes in the crowning of a "King of Congo" and comprises a series of ceremonial acts of a fictional government system with an "ambassador" (*embaixador*), "Secretary of War" (*secretário de guerra*), etc. It is a dramatic resurrection of historical scenes from the time of active diplomatic relations between Portugal and the independent Kingdom of Kôngo. The Congada was at first an internal affair attached predominantly to population groups abducted from northern Angola and the southwest part of Congo. It was also a farce with no real political weight. However, the annual Congada celebration had a strong influence on the solidarity of the Congo groups in Brazil, and it became a sort of political symbol. The whites ridiculed these performances and often misinterpreted the very basics of them.

Today the Congada or "Festa do Congo" still takes place in various Brazilian cities, even in Mato Grosso.[79] A Congada at which African musical instruments from the Congo/Angola environs are played is traditional to Ilhabela, the island at São Sebastião on the coast of São Paulo, and is performed annually in May. It involves the use of a xylophone with gourds and six wooden keys, and the accompaniment of two drums.[80]

In his book *Folclore de São Paulo* (1954, 149-50), Rossini Tavares de Lima published two photos of musical instruments which were used in the 1940s at the Congada at Ilhabela: a *marimba* (with six keys, gourd resonators and carrying handles) and two drums, *tabaque* and *tambú* which can be organologically assigned to the region of Congo and its areas of influence. The connection of the Congada with these instruments from the cultural sphere of the old Kingdom of Kôngo is a sure indication of the direction we must take to explore the history of this Brazilian *folguedo*.

Henry Koster (1816) gave an eye-witness report of a Congada in the first half of the nineteenth century, quoted here from the translation by Rugendas (1835, 26). Koster's description allays any doubt about the significance of the Congada for the Congo descendants in Brazil at that time and of its basis as a recollection of African "cortejos":

> In the month of March the Negroes celebrate the festival of *Nossa Senhora do Rosario.* On this occasion it is their wont to choose a king of Congo if the one who held the honor had died in the course of the year or stepped down for any reason, or when his subjects depose him, which occasionally happens. The Congo Negroes are allowed to choose a king and a queen from their nation, and the choice can be a slave or a free man, and this prince wields a type of power over his subjects that give the whites lots to laugh about. This power is most evident at the Negroes' religious celebrations, like for example the one dedicated to their special patron *Nossa Senhora do Rosario.* The Negro who held this honor in the district of Itamarca (since every district has its own king) wanted to give up the throne due to his advanced age, so they chose a new king, an old slave from the *Amparo* plantation. The old queen had no desire to abdicate and thus preserved her honor.
>
> Early in the morning, the Negro who was to be crowned that day went to the priest to bear witness to his reverence, and said to him jokingly, 'Now then, sir, today I'm going to be your chaplain!' At 11:00 I went with the priest to the church and we soon saw a large crowd of Negroes approaching with flags flying and drums beating: both men and women were wearing the most colorful clothing they could find. When they were close to us, we could identify the king, the queen and the state ministers. The former two wore crowns made of cardboard lids pasted over with gold paper. The king's robe was green, his vest was red and his trousers were yellow—all according to the old style. In his hand he carried a scepter made of gilded wood. The queen wore an ancient of-

ficial's robe made of blue silk. The poor state minister was just as colorfully clad as his master, but he was the only one who had been a bit unlucky with the choice of clothing, for the trousers were much too tight and too short, with the vest on the other hand way too long. The Negroes had to cover the cost of this celebration, so there was a small table set up in the church where the treasurer and a few other officials of the black brotherhood *do Rosario* (of the Rosary) sat in order to collect the donations of those present in a designated tin. The contributions trickled in minimally and very slowly—much too slowly for the taste of the priest, who was eager to be off to his dinner. Thus he impatiently approached the treasurer and assured him that he would not perform the ceremony until all the costs were covered. At the same time he thoroughly chided the Negros around him for their meager enthusiasm to contribute to the production. After he left the group, some of the Negroes started in on some reciprocal assertions and reproaches, accompanied by the most curious gestures and expressions such that were really not appropriate in that holy place. Finally, however, they all agreed. Their black majesties kneeled before the lattice of the altar and the service began. After the mass was over, the king was to be formally installed on his throne, but since the priest was hungry, he had no qualms about shortening the ceremony: he demanded the crown, and then walked with it to the door of the church, where the new king approached him and dropped to his knees. The priest put the crown on his head, placed the scepter in his hand and said: *Agora, Senhor Rey, vai te embora* (Now, Lord King, get away from here!) and quickly went to his house. The Negroes then went with much noisy rejoicing to the *Amparo* plantation where they spent the day and night eating, drinking and dancing.

In a more contemporary report, Rossini Tavares de Lima wrote in his book *Folguedos populares* (1962, 29) about the Congada in the state of São Paulo, which he documented in great detail:

> Everything seems to indicate that Congada (Congado, Congos) as a kind of royal court ceremonial, which can involve two groups representing ambassadors, and in which events of major or minor importance are acted out, even declarations of war, derives from Brazilian festivities of the crowning of a King of Congo. This title is fictitious and was institutionalized in Africa in the fifteenth century, by inspiration from the Portuguese. Perhaps it even favored much more the white Senhor than it did the crowned ruler and his followers, for the simple reason that it was an instrument of the former. It was then spread by enslaved Africans and
>
> Creoles among us, since the seventeenth century and possibly before. At least in 1674, according to documentation found in the church of Rosario in Recife, there was an election of kings and lawyers and other officials to serve Our Lady of the Rosary of Black People.
>
> Actually blacks creating their kings and dancing with joy at festivities for Our Lady of the Rosary and Saint Benedict were also mentioned by Antonil, in 1711 in the work 'Cultura e Opulencia do Brasil'....[81]

There are lasting memories of this one-time powerful African state among those deported from the environs of the old Kingdom of Kôngo, as well as the absolutely equitable relations which it maintained for a long time with Portugal. A political conscience as expression of a cultural identity was traditional in Brazil to such an extent that a sort of fictional Kingdom of Kôngo took hold in the imagination of enslaved Africans on Brazilian soil. This entity had, of course, no political power, since the establishment of *quilombos* did not take place in the south due to the unsuitable ecological conditions. But a dance drama did function in a symbolic way as a psychological niche expressing the dignity and autonomy of one's own group vis-à-vis the foreign group. The "Congada" therewith was born as internal symbolic tradition amongst the enslaved population from Northern Angola and southwest Congo, as well as those who joined this tradition. The Euro-Brazilian authorities were never very pleased about the apparently political contents of such dance dramas; one of the methods to mitigate any danger (as Henry Koster splendidly observed) was to stage these activities—which in any case could only take place inside the Catholic church—as something comical, an approach which the African-Brazilian representatives of this tradition soon internalized.

What may have originally been an attempt to retain in Brazilian surroundings something of the organizational and political structure of historic west Central African states became in the end a farce with lots of theatrical entertainment and elaborate costumes of diverse origins. However, all this was practiced with intense and serious dedication on the part of the representatives of this tradition. The Congada eventually became associated to a great extent with the rites of the Catholic Church, such that late-twentieth century observers believe in all seriousness that it is an offshoot of the French poem of Charlemagne's era, the "Song of Roland."

In addition to the sources already mentioned, Henry Koster (1816) and Johann Moritz Rugendas (1835), historical material on the fictional crowning of African-Brazilian kings can be found in watercolors by Carlos Julião (1740-1811), in particular in the paintings "Cortejo da Rainha negra," "Rei e Rainha negros" and "Coroação de um Rei negro."

Another *folguedo*, the "Bumba-meu-boi," has been examined much less extensively than the Congada. This term, according to Kazadi wa Mukuna, can be translated as "Dance, my bull!"[82] Gilka Corrêa de Oliveira from the Museu do Homem do Nordeste, Recife, noted the following:

> Bumba-meu-boi was one of those plays preferred by the slaves. As it was practiced by them, and by persons in, precarious condition, it showed that the originator (of the play) must have been acting out feelings of social revindication persistent until today.

> The ox is constructed with a scaffolding made of bamboo, lianas and covered with ordinary cloth; the face is generally formed from the skull of an ox or a cow with its horns, or even carved from *mulungu*-wood.

The central figure of this popular drama is the figure of the "bull" (*boi*):

> The play of Bumba-meu-boi is staged in the center of a circle formed by the audience, standing around the performance. According to the manner in which the play evolves and raises interest in the public, the circle will tighten when Mateus and Bastlão (with jokes) or the proper ox (with shoves and kicks) open the performance or initiate its continuation. In some places the ox, after its death, is symbolically cut into pieces to be offered to persons according to their social status and the respect they enjoy in their community.[83]

The "folk drama" or play of Bumba-meu-boi does not refer to one consistent concept in Brazil. Corrêa de Oliveira mentions the following variations, all of which are interesting for us insomuch as they point to various cases of symbolism that are associated with this *folguedo*. These give us a bit of a clue about which directions we may take to explore the African background: "Boi-Bumba" in the region of Amazonas and Pará; "Bumba-meu-boi" in Pernambuco, Alagoas, Bahia, Piaui, Maranhão; "Boi de Matraca," "Boi de Zabumba" and "Boi de Orquestra" in Maranhão; "Boi de Reis" in Acre, Paraíba, Espírito Santo and Ceará; "Boi Surubi" in Ceará; "Boi Calemba" in Rio Grande do Norte; "Boi Maiadinho" in state of Rio; "Boi" or "Boizinho" in São Paulo and Rio Grande do Sul; and "Boi-de-mamáo" in Paraná and Santa Catarina.

The African relationships of this Brazilian *folguedo*, in contrast to the Congada, point not to the area of the Kingdom of Kôngo but rather to Wila (Huíla) province in southwest Angola where there is a strong tradition of livestock raising and where "boi sagrado" (sacred ox) ceremonies are held. The first to report on these magnificent processions was A. F. Nogueira in his

1881 book. Lang and Tastevin (1938) described this festival down to the tiniest detail. Some time ago A. Hauenstein devoted his attentions to the rites and customs connected with cattle-rearing amongst southwest Angolan peoples. The most significant document is, however, a documentary film by Angolan filmmaker Ruy Duarte Carvalho, shot in July 1978 in Wila province (R.P. Angola) and televised by Televisão Popular de Angola under the title *Ondyelwa, Festa do Boi Sagrado* (42 minutes). It is near certain that some elements of the *ondyelwa* dance drama from the Nyaneka cultural area of southwest Angola continue to exist in Bumba-meu-boi of Brazil. This assumption had already been put forward by Edison Carneiro (1937) and Artur Ramos (1937, 1942).

Detailed field research was done on Bumba-meu-boi in Maranhão in 1980-81 by Kazadi wa Mukuna, and recently a film was made. Kazadi recorded a myth about the origins of Bumba-meu-boi in the region of Pindaré, 250 km south of São Luís, the capital city of Maranhão (Mukuna 1986, 110-11). The content analysis of this myth holds the key to insights into this *folguedo*.

> On a cattle farm belonging to a Portuguese man (named Amo—the 'Patron'—in the play) and his wife Dona Maria, there lives the slave Pai Francisco (also called Nego Chico), his pregnant wife (Mãe Catirina) and other slaves. Amo has a favorite ox (called Boi Estrela and Fama Real in the story). One day Mãe Catirina has a craving for ox tongue. She tells her husband about this yearning and says she wants to eat the tongue of her master's favorite animal. Pai Francisco, who is concerned about the life of his unborn child, leads the ox into the forest where he kills it and brings the tongue to his wife. She cooks it and eats it. The next day, Amo notices that his favorite ox is missing and calls together all the shepherds and slaves to ask if anyone has seen it. One of them says that he was watching as Pai Francisco led the 'star ox' (Boi Estrela) into the forest, and that a shot rang out from there moments later. Indeed, the remains of the ox were found when the forest was searched. Enraged at the sight of his dead animal, Amo orders

an Amerindian chief to seize Pai Francisco. Before undertaking this dangerous task the Amerindian chief has a priest bless him. Amo turns to Pai Francisco and orders him to bring the ox back to life, or else to die himself. At this point a Portuguese doctor enters and tries in vain to bring the ox back to life. Then a Shaman, an Amerindian healer, is called. He touches the animal which then actually does get to its feet. Everyone dances with joy the rest of the night (Mukuna 1986. 110-11).

Translated into depth-psychological terms, this myth and its symbolism, according to my analysis, offer a set of important insights. The "Patron" (or the slaveholder, the white man, a father figure) has a secret, a source from which his power and supremacy emanate, a precious possession, a "totem" animal that he could never kill. It symbolizes his innermost being, his self and therewith his powers as a father figure. His dependants, the "children" (or the enslaved Pai Francisco and his wife), can only make their own lives a reality if they symbolically kill the "father" and take possession of his "totem." This is the reason the pregnant woman is yearning for ox tongue and why she puts her man under pressure: If the ox is not killed, then her life, her own future even, is spoilt, and she would have no children. The man carries out her wish; he kills the master's ox. The master realizes this very quickly and sees himself usurped of his powerful identity. He calls together all his "slaves" to find the guilty party. After the perpetrator, the enslaved Pai Francisco, is identified but has already run away, an indigenous person of the land representing the original ownership of the country is supposed to seize him. However, before he acts he needs to undergo a ritual himself to sanction this task. He is blessed by a priest.

The slaveholder, symbolically deprived of his power, demands it be returned by the guilty party to him. He presents Pai Francisco with a choice: he either brings the ox back to life, that is, he reinstates an earlier status, or he himself must die. However, since *both* conditions are not possible as a solution—one can neither turn the clock back nor undo what's been done, or kill one's own dependants for appropriating the father of his "magic"—a symbolic solution is found. The solution is found with the help of an aboriginal, here an Amerindian healer, who, as an original owner of the land, apparently holds the key to justice and answers for the future. The dead ox is *magically* resurrected to an illusionary life. The framework of theater allows that which cannot be restored to be *temporarily* restored. As a symbolic act this has to be repeated over and over again. In this way the conflict is defused.

The theme behind the Bumba-meu-boi myth is appropriation of a power symbol in order to guarantee one's own fertility and prolificacy. The star ox ("boi estrela") with the star symbol for treasure on its forehead stands for the secret source of power of the white slaveholder. The star is simply a symbol of this dynamic radiant source. The ox is a symbol for the strength of the "patron," the protector, the "father" of enslaved Africans—economically, sexually, in every imaginable respect.

The projection of a father figure image by the oppressed onto the oppressor, just as with the projection of a child figure image by the oppressor onto the oppressed is well known to us from colonization psychology. In Brazil the power of this father figure had attained such consummation that, for those oppressed under him, for the symbolic "children" (enslaved Africans, those in bondage), there seemed to be no more procreative future remaining. The power of the father figure did not permit the children any of their own potency. The ability to sire and give birth to offspring was endangered. In order to ensure the prolificacy of their own generation, Pai Francisco, together with his wife, who intuitively recognizes the situation for what it is and unveils the danger early on, must take possession of the magic and the mysterious potency of the slaveholder. In order to survive, the oppressed *must* acquire this power. This can only happen when they *ingest* the potency of the "patron." The symbol of this potency, the star ox, is killed and its heavily symbolic parts (ox tongue) are eaten.

In connection with this interpretation, Moya A. Malamusi was also of the opinion that the wife making a demand of her husband could play a role as a secondary theme of the story. Many African societies have experienced how the woman may lead the man "astray," he said.

The myth itself, as I tried to interpret it, does not actually divulge any information about the origin of Bumba-meu-boi, but rather about its socio-psychological function in a Brazilian context. In this respect the "patron" has taken possession of the magic of resources (symbolized by the ox, which represents wealth in many African cultures), but at the same time, in the eyes of the enslaved Africans subjugated to him, is a "father" who must take care of his "children." The "children" want to get rid of the father, take possession of his property, retain the resources themselves, ingest the magic of the "totem animal" and thus symbolically internalize the father image.

Kazadi's story can be interpreted from several perspectives: depth-psychology, Marxist, etc., and such interpretations yield complementary results. It is also striking that in many etiological myths inherent in African ritual institutions, secret societies, mask games, etc. *analog structures* can be identified. Whatever the issue of conflict may be, the dramatic play that depicts it is a sort of symbolic compromise that functions to remove a conflict, but not solve it. Because the conflict is not actually solved (instead, only through consensus of the people involved, it is continuously deferred), the play (*folguedo*) needs to be constantly repeated. It is similar to the affirmation of a treaty entered upon by two segments of society in conflict with one another. And this is what fuels the further existence of such *folguedos*. In the area of Brazil there is still quite a bit of fuel since the relationship between the "patron" (slaveholder) and the "poor black man" exists to this very day.

The connection to Africa in the myth surfaces only indirectly: namely, that Bumba-meu-boi—as Kazadi wa Mukuna (1986, 111-12) showed in a brilliant analysis—cannot possibly be a creation of the Luso-Brazilian upper class, but can only be a product of enslaved Africans:

> A more detailed look at the contents of the *bumba-meu-boi* shows how the social hierarchy becomes a caricature over time. One makes light of it and steps beyond its limits. From a sociological perspective, the *bumba-meu-boi* was an expression of the downtrodden; it was a possibility for them to question the

authority of the ruling class in colonial Brazil. The play shows that the oppressed, who had no other way to demand their rights, created a theatrical piece in which the despised masters were caricatured and stigmatized. The object of the drama was denunciation of the misbehaving upper class—that is, a satire on the authorities—presented with comedy, music and dance.

Starting with Mãe Catirina's unreasonable request and Pai Francisco's bold consent, this scene of the drama illustrates the ridiculous nature of the masters. The killing of the ox is a crime which will definitely spur the master's anger. On the other hand it demonstrates the high opinion which the lower class held of the strength of the white man's medicine. The Portuguese doctor's attempt fails, however, and only the magic of the Amerindian shaman brings the ox back to life. If *bumba-meu-boi* were a creation of the upper class, there would probably have been only one possible solution—severe punishment of the daring and disobedient slaves and as a consequence the degradation of the race, which is not regarded as human anyways.

One can infer that the enslaved Africans took up ideas which were familiar to them from their indigenous land when creating such plays. The idea of the "boi sagrado" was brought along from Africa as a memory from similar plays, such as were found amongst the Nyaneka of southwest Angola.

There are also parallels from Africa for the motif of the "boi estrela" (star ox), the sacred ox marked with a sign on its forehead. In East Africa, where the culture of shepherding had a great impact on the general culture of the area, there are Wapangwa people belonging to the religious practices surrounding the "holy cow" (*ng'ombe*). This affiliation is marked with a sign on the forehead which all the members of the group have (cf. Kubik 1986c), as shown here:

In Brazil the relationship of patron/slaves was a new situation and so was the socio-psychological response that it elicited. Motifs that had been brought from Africa were retained, but refashioned to express something new, something which related to the situation of the enslaved Africans on the "fazendas." From an historical point of view, Bumba-meu-boi is the continuation of an Angolan *folguedo,* as well as an autonomous new Brazilian creation which was, in a socio-psychological sense, only possible here. Thus Bumba-meu-boi has an African (probably Angolan) component that connects this *folguedo* with rites from the realm of African cattle nomads, as well as a Brazilian component in which the "boi sagrado" (sacred ox) theme acquired an innovative meaning corresponding to the situation of the African in rural Brazil during the time of slavery. Bumba-meu-boi also signaled a response to this situation.

The African-Brazilian fighting games Capoeira and Maculelê also rest on surprising foundations. These were likewise originally an important realm of expression for Brazilian resistance to slavery; here, the possibility of revolt could be explored in all seriousness based on enslaved Africans' memories of training techniques for male youths taught in western Central African initiation schools (*mukanda, ekwenje,* etc.) and traditional tackling techniques.

In their present-day forms, Capoeira and Maculelê are stylized dance and fighting games. In the case of Capoeira two opponents, figures called *golpes* (beats) moving acrobatically and in harmoniously synchronized with the accompanying music, appear to constantly attack and defend without either of them touching each other. The practitioners of this tradition conceptualize it as a game, and not a dance; one says, "o jogo de Capoeira" and not "a dança." Because components of Capoeira are reminiscent of East Asian fighting and defense techniques like judo, kung-fu and karate, recent film productions from Hong Kong have influenced "capoeiristas" at the cinema in Salvador, resulting in the introduction of several kung-fu poses.

Maculelê is a fighting game performed by youths with sticks. While a large group of participating boys forms a circle rhythmically hitting wooden sticks together, two partners feign a battle with two sticks in front of the others. The whole thing is usually accompanied by two tall drums. The one stands upright and is hit with the right hand in a continuous beat; the second one lies on the ground with the performer squatting on the drum and playing passages with both hands.[84]

In Bahia Maculelê is considered a "dance of African origin." It is said to have developed into its contemporary form in Santo Amaro in the state of Bahia. Sticks and bush-knives (facões) were used in this game. According to one source claiming authorship, Maculelê was "created on 2 February 1944 by Paulino Aloisio Andrade." One can compare this assertation with the information accompanying the vinyl recording *Maculelê*.[85] This vinyl recording was recorded in Salvador/Bahia on 4 July 1957 by Aloysio de Alencar Pinto and Allan Lima. The group playing is called Maculelê de Santo Amaro da Purificação, Bahia. Up to this time, writes Alencar Pinto on the record cover, Maculelê was unknown by the majority of folklore scholars.

One can easily believe this latter statement, though the same cannot be said so about the "creation" of Maculelê on 2 February 1944. As so often happens in oral reports about cultural change, such fixed dates are more often that point in time when an old tradition, dressed in new clothing and often carrying a new name, entered public consciousness.

More recently Tiago de Oliveira Pinto also undertook Maculelê field research in the so-called Recôncavo Baiano, the Bahian sugarcane crop area. In a letter dated 15 November 1982, he told me:

> I have several recordings of *maculelê* from Santo Amaro de Puríficação ... the group of this Paulino Aloisio Andrade (called Popó), who Prof. Aloysio de Alencar Pinto so casually called the 'criador'" of the *maculelê*

in his 1957 recording, still exists in Santo Amaro (BA). In fact, Popó (who died in 1969) resurrected a tradition that had languished in forgetfulness (or the subconscious) – a tradition that was likely actively practiced in his youth.

My own impressions of Maculelê and its kinetic-motoric aspects suggest a correlation with the Angolan cultural area. Perhaps my journal notes of 6 October 1975 are the best reflection of my impressions. The group that I saw performed Capoeira and Maculelê. This is not surprising, because as Tiago de Oliveira Pinto (1986a, 150) confirmed, Maculelê is regarded as a prerequisite of later Capoeira instruction. The movement repertoire of African dances is an aspect of African cultures that demonstrates a relatively high level of stability since these patterns of movement, whether they be spatial or not, are so fundamental to African music and dance cultures that changing or eradicating them would be synonymous with the death of the tradition. "At today's event the Central African elements of movement, in particular those I know from Angola, predominated. For anyone at this performance who knows something about African movement systems, it would be impossible not to feel struck by a feeling of *déjà-vu*."[86] Judging from the description of the hip movements in an inserted "Candomblé de Caboclo"—movements practically identical with those of Cokwe boys at a *mukanda* circumcision school in Angola—the following observations emerge: The man with the *agogo* played the sixteen-pulse timeline pattern in the one piece, exactly as I know it from Angola as *kachacha* and which, for example, my friend Vicente dos Santos (in whose personal music culture the Yorùbá element seems to predominate) *cannot* perform. And finally something happened such that I could not believe my eyes. In a piece where each of the usually very youthful participants hold two concussion sticks in their hands, they formed a circle, similar to the way boys in Angola perform *kukuwa* at a *mukanda* initiation school. The drums played during all this and the participants beat the sticks in a perfectly consistent beat. Is this somehow even a holdover from the presumably forbidden circumcision school? This raises an important question. All Angolan ethnicities (with the exception of the Ovimbundu) have circumcision schools for boys. They are circumcised. How could that have gone lost in Brazil? Are there still some holdovers or allusions to this Angolan tradition in Brazil? Perhaps in Maculelê?

The age-segment aspect of Maculelê is apparent in many of its elements. Apart from the physical age of the performing boys, and the fact that Maculelê is a prerequisite for later training in Capoeira as de Oliveira Pinto (1986a, 150) points out. There has been far too little research into Maculelê. But it does appear that in this boys' game two cultural "hang-ups" from Angola and neighboring areas have found a continuation on Brazilian soil: a) the memory of initiation schools, suggested not only in the use of concussion sticks and the age of the boys, but also the way in which the alliance or association of Maculelê and the next pedagogic step, Capoeira, comes across. In Capoeira such associations are called academias, a concept which (not by chance) is borrowed from the pedagogic-educational realm in Brazil; b) the memory of stick fighting as it occurs particularly in the south of Angola amongst the Nkhumbi and Handa, amongst others, in Wila (Huíla) province; this fighting game is called *mpoko* and I documented it in the village of Katengeta in 1965.[87] Two groups of men stand in two lines facing each other. One man steps out from each line, armed with a stick, into the middle and they begin the fight while the other participants clap their hands.

The exponents of the much more famous Bahian fighting game, Capoeira, are completely cognizant of the historical relationship with Angola. The origin of the musical bow (*berimbau de barriga*) which actually was only integrated into the Capoeira game in the twentieth century, can also be traced back to Angola (cf. Kubik 1979a, 33-34). There are not only stylistic dependencies in the *toques* (method of playing, rhythmic patterns) of the *berimbau*; several verbal references to Angola can also be recognized, such as "Banguëla" or "São Bento Grande de Angola." The name of the older form of this fighting game is "Capoeira Angola," in contrast to the so-called "Capoeira Regional" of Mestre Bimba (Rego 1968, 32). Also, it was common to use the expression "a brincar de Angola" for the Capoeira game.[88]

The most comprehensive work written about Capoeira from a Brazilian perspective and including a wealth of data from Bahia is that of Waldeloir Rego (1968). A short, nonetheless very valuable description of Capoeira from the early nineteenth century when these gatherings in the *senzalas* (slave settlements) of plantations still took place can be found in Rugendas 1835. The word "senzala" comes from Kimbundu: *sanzala*, meaning simply "village" or "settlement." Rugendas starts by describing a fight with poles which could be a preliminary form of what one today calls Maculelê, and, at the end of the day, Capoeira.

> It is appropriate here to cite another type of war dance. Two people armed with poles stand facing each other. The skill of the game involves dodging the opponent's thrusts. There is another battle game the Negroes play, *Jogar capoera*, consisting of attempts to knock the opponent down through head-butting with the head resting on the chest. The players dodge each other by parrying and jumping from side to side while thrusting towards each other with their heads almost like bucks. It sometimes happens that the game becomes serious and ends with bloody heads or even the appearance of a knife.[89]

In Rugendas's time Capoeira did not enjoy the graceful reputation it has today. Capoeira was developed on the plantations of Bahia in the eighteenth century (during the time when the majority of the enslaved laborers were of Angolan descent) as a defensive measure and fictional defense training against the slave owners. Participants of the Capoeira fighting games, termed "Jogar Capoëra – Danse de la guerre" by Johann Moritz Rugendas in his illustration caption, gathered in the *senzalas*, quite often at night, to practice various positions and techniques for attack and defense. This usually took place in the absence of weapons, although sometimes with knives. These "positions" developed into what were later called "golpes" and of which every *capoeiristas* masters a wide range of repertoire and terminology. For example, Ginga, Cocorinha, Negatíva, Vôo de Morcego, Tesoura, Rasteíra, Benção, Martelo, Cabeçada, Aú, Rabo de Arraia, etc.[90] A talking drum was used to direct the course of the fighting game, establishing coherence between the musical and kinetic elements. The plantation owners from the Casa Grande, the slaveholders, were aware of course of these practice sessions, but the Angolans in Bahia managed to give them the appearance of a harmless game, "a brincar de Angola." Because it also distracted from aggression within the African group, Capoeira was tolerated. Occasionally this fighting game did, however, raise suspicions but would then be conducted for a while in secret. In a later phase, around the beginning of the twentieth century, after the game had assumed folkloristic traits, and the *berimbau* musical bow had been integrated, Capoeira gatherings were often disbanded by mounted policemen (the so-called "cavalaria") in Bahia. When the police or another stranger was approaching the *roda* (the round dance) of a Capoeira game, the bow-player changed the rhythmic pattern (*toque*); thus all the participants were warned and the whole event was quickly transformed from a fight into a harmless dance. The pattern used to warn of the "cavalaria" is called "cavalaria" and today is still known as "toque de aviso." Many of the musical bow *toques* belong to an extremely old Angolan tradition.[91]

Just as various African vocabularies continued to exist in Brazil, Capoeira was also a product of psychological resistance against the slave owners and colonists. It was possible using language to communicate with each other without the knowledge of the senhor. Thanks to the secret unarmed training called Capoeira, the utopic possibility of a general uprising could be entertained. Only in their outward appearance were the Angolans the docile and subordinate people described in the literature of the time.[92] The Angolans appear to have cultivated a deeply-rooted black consciousness in Brazil using language to a greater degree than the West Africans, who were more likely to openly demonstrate resistance. In those places were Capoeira was forced underground, or where the true character of this fight-training had to remain concealed, people came up with appropriate ways of behaving so as to transform it into a harmless dance game at any time.

As social change in Brazil in the late nineteenth century increasingly diluted the original meaning of Capoeira training, Capoeira began to lose more and more of its original character. Two new trends appeared. As happens rather often when a planned revolution is aborted or becomes hopeless, the originally revolutionary spirit slips into criminality: armed gangs spring up. Capoeira appears to have undergone such a phase in the second half of the nineteenth century. Tiago de Oliveira Pinto (1986b, 148-49) sums up as follows:

> Because the *capoeira* fighting technique was often employed in quarrels between rival groups during the past century and after the abolishment of slavery in 1888 -- above all in the cities of Salvador and Rio -- and because it just as often resulted in some spilt blood, the police were always trying to suppress the practice of *capoeira*. From time to time they were able to disband so-called 'gangs' (*maltas*), roughly from around 1865 to 1870, when many *capoeiristas* were forcibly recruited for the war against Paraguay. It was said that on the battlefield they successfully gave their all for the fatherland.
>
> Around the end of the nineteenth century two large rival *capoeira* groups had formed in Rio de Janeiro. To some extent, their members entered the services of politicians and were entrusted with the task of intimidating political opponents: on some occasions they attacked with hidden knives and razor blades. Only around the turn of the century was there a dreaded police chief Sampaio Ferraz, who was successful in putting a end to the belligerent *maltas* in Rio.

The second trend which ultimately continued through the present day was the development of the variation "o jogar de capoeira," presented as a game. In this phase musical instruments were adopted from widely varied African-Brazilian traditions. Still associated today with Capoeira, these instruments provide its accompaniment. First and foremost is the Angolan gourd-resonated musical bow, which was very popular during the nineteenth century as a solo instrument in Rio de Janeiro, where it was known as "oricongo."

As we identified in our research in Brazil and Angola, it is derived directly from Angolan bows that were known under the names of *hungu, ungu, lukungu* (from which "oricongo" is derived).⁹³ Still recognized in Brazil as late as the nineteenth century, the Angolan terms are by and large forgotten today, and the instrument is now called *berimbau* or, more precisely, *berimbau de barriga*.

In Rio de Janeiro, as in Angola, the gourd bow was played without a simultaneously sounded woven rattle (*caxixi*). In contrast, in Bahia the latter is indispensable for contemporary performance of the Bahian *berimbau*—the simultaneous playing of the bow and rattle likely having been developed there. The woven rattle *caxixi* is probably of West African origin; rattles of this construction and size are found amongst the Ewe in Togo and Benin (Dahomey) as well as with northeast Nigerian people. The principle of the *caxixi*, based on a gourd whose hard external surface is turned inside out, is indeed known in the Congo/Zaïre cultural region; however, there such basket rattles are larger and have a handle. There are reports from Brazil of this latter type as well, in particular from the state of São Paulo where it is known as "angoia" (Araújo 1973, 133).

Caxixi (pronounced Kashishi) is onomatopoeic. The instrument was probably first named by Angolan descendants in Bahia in the context of the Capoeira tradition. The name can be broken down morphologically as follows: *ka-* is a diminutive prefix; *-shishi* is ideophonic and symbolizes the sound of the rattle. Thus, *caxixi* makes perfect sense: the little thing that goes "shi-shi-shi..." in its sound.

It is still unresolved as to whether the combination of *berimbau* and *caxixi*, despite their apparent development in Bahia, was inspired by a fine thread emanating from Angolan or other African models. Up to now I have not come across the combination in Angola. I know of only one area of Africa where there is a comparable combination: Burundi and its surroundings. The gourd bow *muduri* is played in a position similar to that of the *berimbau*, though with a different left-hand finger grip. Between the index and ring fingers of his right hand the musician holds a thin stick with which he hits the instrument's single string, and, in the same hand holds a second stick with a small spherical rattle made of a dried *oncoba spinosa* (snuff-box tree) fruit casing fastened to the upper end. When playing the bow the *berimbau* players combines the use of string and rattle beats. The rattle used by the Barundi, however, has nothing in common with the *caxixi* in terms of organology.

The etymology of the terms for the two African-Brazilian fighting games under discussion, Maculelê and Capoeira, remains unclear today. If the expression Maculelê does hold a trace of Bantu-language elements, then it would be *ma-*, interpreted as cumulative prefix, and *ku-le-le* most likely as onomatopoeia, the expression of the beating of the sticks. Maculelê (*makulele*) might in this case then mean: the concussion sticks themselves (plural) and the beating sounds that are made by them. I posed the following question to my colleague, Moya A. Malamusi: "If you came to a random Brazilian village with African descendants and someone suddenly said *makulele makulele*, what would you, with no knowledge of specific language remnants, think was meant?" Moya thought for a moment and then said: "I would think that it referred to some games, *masewera*."[94]

It is considerably more difficult to get behind the etymology of the word "Capoeira" (pronounced *kapwera*). Accordingly, myriad speculative interpretations crop up in Brazilian literature. Waldeloir Rego (1968, 27-29) offers an index of attempted derivations, including those from Amerindian languages. The most obvious solution still seems to be the Portuguese meaning "chicken-cage." Enslaved Africans regularly used these to transport poultry to town to be sold. It is a sort of large bucket: Capoeira—"Espécie de cêsto feito de varas, onde se guardam capões, galinhas e outras aves" (Kind of basket made of sticks, where you keep capons [castrated roosters], chickens and other birds) (cf. Rego 1968, 27).[95] Antenor Nascentes (see Rego 1968, 25) supports the following theory: "A etimologia que eu hoje aceito para capoeira é a que vem no livro de Brasil Gerson sôbre as ruas do Rio de Janeiro. Os escravos que traziam capoeiras de galinhas para vender no mercado, enquanto êle não se abria, divertiam-se jogando capoeira. Por uma metonímia *res pro persona*, o nome da coisa passou para a pessoa com ela relacionada" (The etymology which I accept today for the term capoeira is the one proposed in the book by Brasil Gerson on street life in Rio de Janeiro. The enslaved Africans who were carrying chicken coops on their heads for sale in the market, used to amuse themselves by playing a wrestling game, while the market was still closed. Due to *metonymy res pro persona*, the name of the objects was passed on to the activities of the persons associated with it.).

As obvious as this theory may be, there is one thing it does not explain: how did this correlation come about? In light of the socio-psychological background of Capoeira at the time of slavery, Capoeira could probably also have functioned as a code word which enslaved Africans used for their secret fighting training (cf. also Kubik 1979a, 29). Is it coincidence or an expression of an implicit, still existent association that the Brazilian army gave one of their manoeuvres the code name "Operação Capoeira"?

It is also strange that no Brazilian authors seemed to think that a Bantu word phonemically identical with the Portuguese "capoeira," and one which the Angola enslaved Africans knew, could have existed. The enslaved Africans from Angola in this bilingual setting would certainly have at least used such a double meaning to their own advantage. There are countless such bilingual examples from Africa. The orthographic transcription of "capoeira" in Angolan languages would be *kapwera* or *kapwela* (in some of these languages "l" and "r" are one and the same phoneme and thus are interchangeable).

If dealing with a noun, then the plural of the Angolan word would be either *tupwera* or *vapwera*; if a verb, then *kapwera* is the imperative form, and the infinitive is *kukapwera*. Emil Pearson, born in 1897 and who lived in southeast Angola from 1922, responded to my question as follows: "Kapuela (Kapwela) is a verb in the Mbunda language and means 'to clap hands'. Rhythmic clapping of the hands often accompanies games and especially shows of athletic prowess, and, carried to another region, could easily become a noun in its usage."[96]

This is an aspect that I mention only for the sake of completeness. There is not one iota more probability in it than there is in the Capoeira "chicken-cage" theory. What cannot be determined here is that the word Capoeira concretely derives from some coincidentally similar-sounding Bantu word; I advised against this kind of linguistic relational research in an earlier chapter. However, in light of the psychological situation of African descendants in Brazil in the eighteenth and nineteenth centuries, we see a concrete possibility that the Brazilian word Capoeira could perhaps have been a merging of two concepts able to be used as code as easily as one turns over a coin: that Capoeira was an expression with a double-meaning with which one tried to conceal something that belonged to the African experience.

Urbano Fernando de Leite, the leader of the Congada of Vila Bela da Santíssima Trindade, with our African colleague Donald Kachamba, who is wearing a Congada headdress. Vila Bela da Santíssima Trindade, Mato Grosso, 2 November 1980. Photo by Moya A. Malamusi.

Performance of "Bumba-meu-boi" at Mardi Gras in Recife. This group from the interior of Pernambuco state also calls the ox "Boi-teimoso," the stubborn ox. A person is costumed as the "boi." Photo by Tiago de Oliveira Pinto, Recife, 1987.

Boys aged around six to twelve with concussion sticks (Brazilian: "grima," from "esgrima," the art of sword-wielding) in Maculelê group training. Photo by Tiago de Oliveira Pinto, Ilha-do-Dendê (Bahia), 1984.

Boys in an initiation school in Angola with concussion sticks. This institution is called ekwenje amongst the Nkhumbi and Handa. The boys spend several months in seclusion, where they are instructed. Near the village of Mambondwe, Wila (Huíla) province, Southwest Angola, July 1965. Photo by G. Kubik.

Documentation of a simulated fight with sticks in Southwest Angola. This is called mpoko. The participating men all have herdmens' crooks in their hands and hit each other with them in these duels. Village: Katengeta, Província de Huíla, Southwest Angola, July 1965. Photo by G. Kubik (F 51).

These are the two (see also next image) of the oldest iconographic renderings of Capoeira, according to our current knowledge. The top picture (a) is not identified by the author; however, it is definitely a "Capoeira" fighting game that is taking place with vaguely recognizable accompaniment and spectators including the obligatory fruit vendor. It should actually still be possible to identify the location of this scene in Salvador/Bahia.

The second photo (b) is substantially more detailed and places "Capoeira" directly in front of the walls of the house of a "senhor." The fighting game is immediately recognizable: "Jogar Capoëra ou danse de la guerre," reads the short caption. The movements and actions of the two "capoeiristas" facing each other are clearly being directed and controlled by the drummer in the Napoleonic-era uniform hat who is holding the drum between his legs and beating with his hands. Numerous spectators of various professions are present, including the pineapple vendor with the basket on his head and others, some of them wearing stylish clothing, like the intensely engaged man at the left wearing the top hat. Reproduction from Johann Moritz Rugendas, 1835.

Performance of a fighting game on the plaza in front of the Mercado Modelo in Salvador/Bahia. Several passersby have formed a circle and give small monetary gifts to the group when they finish a round. The capoeiristas in this photo is in a characteristic striking position (golpe), known as "Aú." Salvador/Bahia, 20 September 1975. Photo by G. Kubik (A 178).

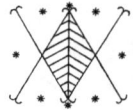

THE AFRICAN-BRAZILIAN RELIGIONS: A RELIGIOUS SYNCRETISM?

African-Brazilian religions and practices of communication with the transcendental world belong to the subjects that particularly draw the attention and awaken the interest of many researchers: Candomblé in Salvador/Bahia, Xangô in Recife and Umbanda" in São Paulo, Rio de Janeiro and other cities in southern Brazil. A particular emphasis of studies was on the religious manifestations of the Yorùbá culture, with its "pantheon" of the òrìṣà in Bahia, whereas the religious traditions of Bantu population descendants in Brazil were studied on a less scholarly basis, instead remaining more a subject addressed in popular literature devoted to occultism and parapsychology. Fernando Albuquerque Mourão remarked regarding this noticeable stratification:

> Our ideas and our knowledge relating to the African continent still leave much to be desired. The concentration of studies about 'black' people either on questions of origin, or the so-called religious syncretism, principally in Bahia, has contributed to a systematic distortion of the problem. Our bibliography on 'black' people clearly shows that most valuable studies were focusing on Bahia or Recife, searching for origins to explain an African-Brazilian syncretism. But when it comes to studies referring to other regions such as São Paulo or Rio de Janeiro, 'blacks' are seen only as part of a class society, and questions of (cultural) origins and the African heritage do not stir any interest in the observers.... In addition, 'Bantu' are systematically portrayed as carriers of a poor mythology, imitative of 'Sudanic' or Christian ideas. The underlying concept is a conviction that in the

past Africa was only absorbing influences, i.e. from other civilizations, notably in the 'Sudanic' region. Such concepts are based on prejudices inherited from colonialism and on the absence of a comprehensive awareness of the variety of African cultures in their own contexts.[97]

So-called syncretism—a merging and equalization of sacred Christian figures with characters from the Yorùbá religion "orixa"—held a particular fascination for researchers in Bahia.

In the Candomblé religious communities of Bahia, the following equivalents are generally accepted: Ogum is St. Anthony; Ossaim is St. Benedict; Oxóssi is St. George; Xangô is St. Jerome; Omolu is St. Lazarus (or St. Rochus); Oxumaré is St. Bartholomew; Iansã is St. Barbara; Oxum is Our Lady of Candelária or also the Virgin Mary; Yemanjá is Our Lady of Aparecida; Nanã is St. Anne; Oxalá is Our Lord of Bomfim (the son of the Christian God). The religions festivals of Bahia, like the famous water processions for the Yemanjá or Janaina (mythical figure of a water-bound being with the torso of a woman and the lower body of a fish) on the occasion of the annual *Dia de Iemanjá* on December 8 have been extensively documented.[98]

As already implied in my remarks on *folguedos* in the preceding section, African cultures in Brazil showed prevalent tendencies to manifest themselves within the oppressor's protective cloak and the framework of his institutions. In the case of the Congada, it is the association of this *folguedos* with "Nossa Senhora do Rosário," the black patron saint, or "black mother of God" in the context of Brazilian Catholicism. African heritage penetrated the most sacred institutions of the whites. African religious perceptions were projected onto concepts and rites of the Catholic Church. They were adjusted to fit and thus they won approval. This led to a development like the one in Bahia where there was, as it were, a Catholic saint on the front side of Bahian Catholicism and a Yorùbá òrìṣà on the back. They became identical with each other. And this coin can be arbitrarily turned over like a code depending on the situation. Borrowing from the concept of code-switching in sociolinguistics, one could call this "symbol-switching." But it could not really be termed syncretism.

In reality, the African-Brazilian religious practices are not syncretic at all. They are African religions which were, thanks to the Portuguese language and the domain of Catholic concepts, translated for outsiders into a non-African code—to fulfil the need "how to explain to the whites what òrìṣà means." The best way was to compare òrìṣà with what the whites call "saints" in their Catholic church. The African-Bahians were bilingual from early on and versed in the religion of the senhor. The outcome of this cultural contact was not syncretism but rather, quite simply, that the religious system of the òrìṣà was from then on accessible in two languages—in Yorùbá (with Yorùbá concepts) and in Portuguese/Brazilian (with fairly comparable Catholic concepts). Yorùbá became the liturgical language in Candomblé just as Latin was in Catholicism.

According to Peter Clarke (in Murray 1981, 38), the Yorùbá religion—as it still exists today amongst 40 million Yorùbá-speakers in western Nigeria and the Republic of Benin—embodies a system of spiritual or quasi-spiritual beings on four levels. At the upper end of the spectrum is *Olódùmare*, the highest being, also called Ọlọrun (literally, owner of the heavens). Next in line are the òrìṣà, often inaccurately translated as "gods," but categorized by rank. Under this level, Ọbàtálá is the next most important figure. This divinity is also called Òrìṣànlá, literally meaning "the great òrìṣà"; the term is an blending of òrìṣà and *nlá* (large). Ọbàtálá refers in Yorùbá mythology to an active force that enabled *Olódùmare* to execute the achievement of creation. According to a myth published by Timi of Èdè (Laoye II 1959, 6), Ọbàtálá descended from Heaven after creating the world to dance to his four wives' clapping. Finally he had four drums made from òmòn wood, and he named these after his wives. This is the second level.

On the third level of spiritual beings are figures which can be interpreted as deified ancestors, such as Ṣàngó (in Brazilian, "Xangô"), once king of the Yorùbá city Ọyò, and, at the same time, thunder and lightning. On the fourth level follow spirits which are connected with natural phenomena, like *Onile* ("divinity of the earth").

Ulli Beier (1982, 3) noted that òrìṣà should be regarded as a complex concept that must be regarded in various ways simultaneously. As in other African religions (e.g. in the Bwiti religious practices of Gabon), the òrìṣà is perceived by entranced priests as a colorful form in which several interwoven "pictures" (visual, acoustic, olfactory, etc.) of the material world appear. Ulli Beier (1982: 4) formulates this as follows:

> It is a force of nature (thunder, gale, river, cliffs, iron or sea) and simultaneously of man (warrior, founder of cities, hunter, smith or sorcerer); at the same time it is symbolized by animals or plants or colors. Shango is thunder and at the same time a tragic hero figure from the kingdom of Oyo: a king who took his own life out of disappointment over his subjects. His symbol is the ram, whose head-butts can hit us lightning-fast. The human who is close to Shango occupies himself with the powers he embodies. He embellishes himself with his colors (red and white) and protects himself with rituals and magical medicines from powers which don't comply with his principles ... every god is also a kind of archetype and the human becomes ever more similar to his òrìṣà as the god 'rides' the human during repeated states of trance.

The Yorùbá religion and its broad palette of transcendental beings called òrìṣà is certainly not unique in West Africa in terms of its foundation. It turns up again in a fairly identical structural form in Fon in Dahomey (Yorùbá's western neighbor) and Togo under the name *vodu*. Due to a lack of exact knowledge of central West African correlations, many misunderstandings have recently spread about the *vodu* religion, which also established itself in the Americas (in particular in Haiti), due to deported peoples from the so-called slave coast. It is even been said that *vodu* is of African diaspora origin and spread from the Caribbean over to West Africa.

The concept *vodu* in the Fon language of Dahomey (present-day Republic of Benin, and not to be confused with the historic Benin in present-day Nigeria) correlates almost completely in its semantic scope with the Yorùbá concept of òrìṣà. Just as with the Yorùbá people—where a child is dedicated to a certain òrìṣà, determined by an oracle, at an early age—the Fon and Ewe peoples, in the cases where they have taken on the *vodu* religion, are dedicated to a *vodu*. The palette of *vodu* beings is indeed rather different from that of the òrìṣà; however there are quite a few figures which are practically identical, such as Hɛvyɛso (thunder and lightning divinity) amongst the Fon people corresponding to Ṣàngó amongst the Yorùbá, or *Legba* amongst the Fon to Ẹsu amongst the Yorùbá.

The Yorùbá figure of the *bàbálòrìṣà* corresponds to that of the Fon *vodusi*. The linear correlation of many religious concepts of the Yorùbá to the Fon and vice-versa led to coalescences of the òrìṣà and *vodu* religions in the Americas; however, depending on the dominance of one or the other group, the terminology of one or the other language always established itself. If one were to employ the word syncretism anywhere at all, it would describe the melding of these West African religions with each other due to an identity established long ago.

Thus there indeed came about a syncretism in the Bahian Candomblé religion between the religious ideas of the two neighboring populations of the "Nagô" people (with ethnic subgroups of the Ketu and Ijexá) and the "Gêge" people (identical with the Ewe and Fon). It was perhaps because the "Nagô" were stronger in numbers that Yorùbá terminology soon dominated. Ewe elements are, however, still present in contemporary Candomblé--and not only that of the "Nação Gegê," presiding today over four temples in Salvador/Bahia—but also in others.[99]

The Candomblé religious centers in the state of Bahia are mainly concentrated in the urban areas, above all in the capital city Salvador/Bahia. One reason for this may be attributed to the fact that the òrìṣà religion was originally associated with traditional city-states in West Africa, so it was also an urban phenomenon there. The temples of Candomblé are called *terreiros* (courts/sacred places). Most of them are found in Salvador in peripheral, less accessible parts of town. They can be broken down into the following "ethnic" traditions: 660 belong to the "Nação Ketu" (Yorùbá subgroup), 271 to the "Candomblé-de-Cabocìo" (dedicated to local, formerly Amerindian spirit beings), 350 to the "Congo-Angola" group and four to the "Nação Gegê."[100]

We can certainly presume that the Yorùbá religion in its various forms in Nigeria as well as in neighboring Dahomey has changed since the sixteenth century, and, all the while, also in those areas of the Americas to which it was exported. Here it should be noted that the export of the Yorùbá religion to Bahia cannot be regarded as something like a one-time transplant, but instead was constantly being fortified through new arrivals from Nigeria up until the moratorium on enslaved African importation in 1851. So there were continual updates of recent developments from the African side. And from 1851, the contacts persevered in one form or another. Nonetheless, the separation of the òrìṣà religion from that in its region of origin for a span of somewhat more than 100 years, as well as the heterogeneous influences that rubbed against it in Brazil, did lead to substantial changes. In the 1980s, the Brazilian manifestations are indeed different to those in Nigeria on many points. Tiago de Oliveira Pinto (1986b, 161-62) summarized the current situation as follows:

> The number of Yorùbá divinities [venerated] in Brazil is substantially smaller than in West Africa. In the *candomblé* [religious communities], for example, there are only up to sixteen *orixás* (the usual spelling in Brazil for the Yorùbá word òrìṣà) invoked and [venerated]. However, the hierarchy of these supernatural beings still exists to a certain extent in Brazil. The four levels described above do have counterparts amongst the relational ranks of the *orixás* and the other beings. Although the respective myths surrounding the *orixás* and their relative associations (depending on region, *nação* and even community) are, of course, interpreted differently, the most broadly ranging relative relationships in the *candomblé* world of the 'gods' are presented in excerpts in the diagram [below].

> This simplified 'family tree' demonstrates a certain correlation between the four hierarchical ranks found in Africa and the various generations of the divine beings found in Brazil. As a matter of principle, Oxalá (Orixalá), corresponding to the African Obatalá, can be regarded as the epicenter of the sys-

tem, equivalent to 'Ego.' His father Olorum, as in Africa, prevails over all beings and over creation itself. He is the lord of all life and even in *candomblé* he is neither directly invoked nor worshiped. His son Oxalá is known as the highest of all *orixás*, as well as the *orixá* of creation. His first wife Nanã and his second wife Yemanjá are known as the *orixás* of procreation. The second hierarchical rank, to the extent that one can say that in Brazil, is occupied here exclusively by Oxalá. Other than in the African system, the large group of the remaining *orixás*, Oxalá's wives and children, comprise the third level.

On the fourth and last level of the *candomblé* supernatural world is arguably the most contradictory being. This is Exu, the intermediary between the earthly and the *orixá* worlds. Some legends say that Exu is a product of the marriage between Oxalá and Yemanjá. Exu holds an important position as follows: news and supplications are relayed by him from one world to the other; it is he who takes care that offerings are actually accepted by the appropriate *orixás*. He is especially feared because he appears not only as a protector, but also carries out multiple punishments of those who do not obey the religious commandments.

Genealogy of the Orixás in Candomblé

```
                         Olorum
  I.                       △
  ─────────────────────────┼─────────────────────────
  II.                   Creation
       Procreation         │              Procreation
                Nanã     Oxalá    Yemanjá    Orania(Odudua)
                 ○━━━━━━━▲━━━━━━━━○━━━━━━━━━━△
  ─ ─ ─ ─ ─ ─ ─ ─ ─ ┼ ─ ─ ─ ─ ─ ─ ─ ┼ ─ ─ ─ ─ ─ ─ ─
                    │               │
                □  △  ○           △   △
  III.       Oxumare Omolu Irokô  Ogun Xangô
         ┌────┬────┬────┬────┬────┐
         △    △    ○    ○    ○    ○
       Oxossi Ossaim Obá Iansã Eua Oxum
         △
  IV.   Exu
```

(Diagram adapted from Tiago de Oliveira Pinto 1986b, 162).

Regarding religious practice in Bahia—in contrast to that in Nigeria—Tiago de Oliveira Pinto adds the following to his preceding remarks (1986b, 163):

> Unlike the Yorùbá in West Africa, where every òrìṣà is designated a different [sacred] site, shrine and priests, all *orixás* in Brazil are [venerated] in the same *terreiro*. However, each *candomblé* temple is dedicated to a certain *orixá*, each of which is assigned to a different space on the *terreiro* property. In any case it should be noted that the following tendency may be observed in the structure of the divinity-world in *candomblé* in Brazil: simplification and standardization of West African creation mythology comes to the fore, just as may be observed in other areas as well, and in this case, not the least, manifests itself in the reduction of the number of revered *orixás*.

A considerable amount of literature already exists on the topic of Candomblé. European religious scholars have also recently turned increased attention to this theme. For one, Allard Willemier Westra, from the Institute for the Study of Religion at the Vrije Universiteit in Amsterdam, has undertaken several study trips to Brazil, including 1978/79 to Bahia, where he researched the Candomblé religion in the small city of Alagoinhas. Westra was particularly interested in "problem-solving" in the framework of the Candomblé belief system and its followers' perception of the world. In other words, he looked at the style and manner in which one attempts to solve one's everyday material and spiritual personal problems with the help of Candomblé.[101]

My first impression of a Candomblé event with a Nagô/Yorùbá group is reflected in the following journal entries from 20 October 1974:

> With the aim of visiting an authentic Candomblé, we went yesterday to the Sociedade Protectora dos Desinvalidos, founded in 1832, together with Manoel de Almeida Cruz and Roberto Santos from the Núcleo Cultural Afro-Brasileiro. The Sociedade, one of the first black movements in Bahia, was originally founded to purchase the freedom of enslaved Africans... First we visited a smaller event in a mud-walled house outside of town where the participants stood knee deep in front of the drums and dancers. Two solo dancers made small rolling shoulder movements and deliberate slow two-steps in the Yorùbá dance style... The Candomblé event at the second site was much more spectacular: we stood in a huge room with parquet floors and wall paintings of Iemanjà and the terrible white knight (São Jorge). The greatest surprise for my friend Donald Kachamba was that there was a giant, gaudily attractive color painting of Iemanjà or Janaina. It was placed behind an altar-like construction with a huge sofa on which an almost regally dressed old woman sat -- the leader of the group, assisted by two more women to her left and right. Iemanjà is half woman/half fish and wears a crown on her head. Donald immediately nudged me and said: Mami Wata! He knew this concept from

West Africa (Nigeria), where there is a similar figure in popular mythology—all the way from the coast, far off towards Cameroon and into the Central African Republic. The Pidgin English expression 'Mami Wata' (Mamywater or mother of the water, of the sea) has even established itself in French-speaking regions of West Africa. A young man who enters a personal relationship with Mami Wata and falls for her will acquire tremendous riches and fame, but at the end of it all, Mami Wata takes him away with her to the sea. In particular one says in West Africa that famous artists and musicians can thank their relationship with Mami Wata for their fame and fortune...[102] All the women were dressed in sparkling, flowing gowns. The woman sitting in front of the painting of Janaina had a rattle in her hand with which she occasionally scattered 'sprays' of her blessings in the direction of the audience. Three drums were playing: *rum*, *rumpi* and *lé* as well as a double bell (*agogô*) of the type for sale at the Mercado Modelo. The group of drummers stood to the right of the altar (seen from our perspective) and was set up in just the way that our acquaintance, the painter Descartes Gadelha, had drawn: in the order of *agogô*, *lé*, *rumpi* and *rum*. This corresponded to the functions of these instruments. A timeline pattern was being kept on the *agogô* bell, with each system corresponding to a certain òrìṣà. It was the task of the *rumpi* player to play this same pattern with two sticks on his drum, including complementary rhythms to fill the gaps; the right-hand stick beats together with the bell. The *rum* player is the lead drummer. Since taping was not allowed, we had to make our recordings clandestinely; at first from outside through the building's window, as well as later when Donald and I mingled amongst the crowd standing by the dance floor, I hid the recorder in a bag on the floor between my feet and Donald held the microphone up in the direction of the singers and dancers, at a distance of about 7 meters. We had arrived fairly early at this Candomblé; it was about 10 pm. Only as time went by did the atmosphere "heat up," fireworks were shot off and regally dressed women appeared from a door of the wardrobe behind the altar, with the Ṣàngó-sign (the X symbol) on a hilt in their hands, and they danced into a circle formation and then back again in a counter-clockwise direction.

The dance movements consisted of slow two-steps 12 [r . l r . . l . r l . .] to the rhythm of the Yorùbá beating-pattern, 12 pulses for the agogô: 12 [x . x . x x . x . x . x]. Since there was also no photography permitted, Descartes Gadelha made the adjacent drawings. The song, partly with Yorùbá texts, was performed by the dancing women and the lead drum (*rum*) player. The possession of some of the participating women only took place around midnight."[103]

Without a doubt, the Yorùbá element dominated in this "Nagô" Candomblé. Generally speaking, however, the numerous non-Yorùbá elements in the Candomblé religious practices in Bahia, even those which are nominally "Nagô," cannot be ignored. The most striking elements are the three drums *rum, rumpi* and *lé*. According to personal correspondence from Valentine Ojo, June 1977, drum names like this are not recognized in Yorùbá territory. It is not yet known where these terms originated, although the term *agogô* for bell comes from the Yorùbá language and, for example in the Ondo dialect, refers to a single bell (cf. Ojo 1976). The revealing feature of the three drums in Candomblé and the key to the localization of their West African connections is the way in which the skin is stretched, namely the "cord-and-peg tension," a technique characteristic of drums from the Nagô and Gêge groups (de Oliveira Pinto 1986c, 16). This is the significant feature facilitating an analysis to trace this drum type back to Africa. As a rule, *technologies* are retained until the point that they may be replaced by new technologies. Being grounded in innovative invention, technologies have a highly unique character in terms of form. On the Brazilian scene, the "cord-and-peg tension" technique (cf. Wieschhof 1933), in connection with the presence or absence of certain time-line patterns (cf. Kubik

1979a), is a further diagnostic feature in the music domain for historical connections to pinpointed regions of Africa. According to the sources known to us, this technique is only found in a section of the Guinea coast of West Africa, in an outlined area including for the most part Ghana, Togo and Dahomey, and adjacent areas of Nigeria. Therefore it is probable that it has a "Gêge" background (that is, including Ewe and neighboring ethnicities) as its West African area of origin. This is backed up by the fact that certain drum-skin clamping techniques are apparently strictly correlated with the cultural aspects of surviving African "nações" in Brazil. An instance of this is the "wedge-and-ring tension" technique originating in central Africa and West Africa over to the Niger Delta, characteristically found amongst Congo/Angola Candomblé groups in Salvador.

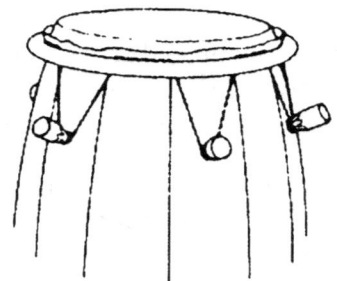 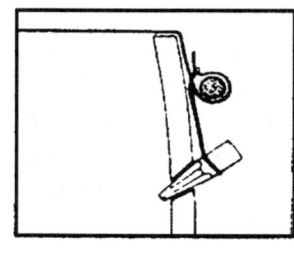

"Cord-and-peg tension" on Candomblé drums of the Nagô and Gêge people in Bahia (Illustration reproduced from de Oliveira Pinto 1986c, 16).

The "cord-and-peg tension" method of stretching the drum skin consists of a combination of a ring, under which the stretched skin is rolled up, spanning the upper circumference of the drum; a rope passed through rows of holes perforated in the rolled-up layers of the skin perimeter; and wooden pegs inserted at an angle into the body of the drum. The rope is wound and pulled tightly around the pegs. This type of stretching is still found on many Candomblé drums in Bahia. The wooden pegs are sometimes replaced with metal parts in mass-production or in manufacture involving drum mass-production technique. Other elements evident in the same Ewe/Akan-speaking area of Guinea (a concentrated historical place of reference for the *rum, rumpi* and *lé*) are the tall shape of these drums and the playing method using sticks for the *rumpi* and *lé*, and partially for the *rum*. Drums of today such as the *atsimevu* drums of the Ewe in Ghana have much in common with the Candomblé drums of Brazil in terms of form and beating techniques. Certainly they all belong to the same larger family from which also the *rum, rumpi* and *lé* originated.

Since continued existence of musical traditions is essentially dependent on non-musical contexts, Yorùbá music in Brazil retained its identity to a great extent thanks to its association with African-Brazilian religious communities of Yorùbá origin. Occasionally one still finds patterns and drum phrases in Bahia that in the meantime have disappeared in Nigeria and Dahomey, or which are regarded there as ancient.

Yorùbá religious songs have established themselves and retained their identity even outside Bahia and far into the south of Brazil. Religious ideas of Yorùbá origin infiltrated the Umbanda religious communities in the south. From the moment where Umbanda religious songs were sung for Yorùbá òrìṣà, distinctly Yorùbá stylistic features started to appear in the intonation and melodic intervals. An example is the songs performed by Sr. Aparecido Morato from Vila Maria Alíce in Paraná. These demonstrate definite Yorùbá stylistic features. The songs are from an Umbanda association to which he belongs. We recorded him singing the songs in April 1979 on the occasion of our visit to his relative Sr. Caxias in Capivari. The Yorùbá words in the text aside, I was quite well acquainted already with the thoughtful, syllable-by-syllable placement of words—of an almost monosyllabic feel—within a tonal language style. I had experienced this with Duro Ladipo's compositional technique in Nigeria (Oshogbo 1960), and the similarity in the placement of the text was indeed astounding. The pentatonic tonal system likewise distinctly differentiated Morato's songs from the rest of Umbanda repertoire. The remarks on the recordings made by Sr. Morato at the end of his presentation confirmed my hunches: all the recorded songs were dedicated to Yorùbá òrìṣà (or orixá); amongst others, songs for "Xangô" (no. 14) and Ogúm" (no. II/1), or Ṣàngó and Ogun in Yorùbá orthography.[104] Sr. Morato is the nephew of the 82-year-old leader of a Batuque dance group from Capivari, Sr. Benedito

Caxias, whose own cultural pocket demonstrates absolutely no further Yorùbá cultural elements.

The function, contents and history of the so-called Umbanda religions in southern Brazil are frequently misunderstood. It must be emphasized here that every examination of Umbanda which is limited to Brazil will, from a purely Luso-Brazilian standpoint, yield distorted results. Any historical examination of Umbanda firstly demands a comprehensive knowledge of what Umbanda means in its indigenous Angola before any interpretation can be made of its Brazilian aspects. Such words as "trance," "rites," "cult," black magic," "consecration," etc. are seldom absent from descriptions of African-Brazilian religions. These are words that predictably stimulate the unconscious psyche and prompt fantasies amongst European and North American readers to the extent that the author can save himself the trouble of delivering hard facts. It suffices to let just one of these words drop in a well-chosen moment to achieve a desired psychological conditioning effect on his readers.

Also interesting from a socio-psychological point of view is the amount of pseudo-scholarly literature being written in Brazil about Umbanda. In Rio de Janeiro and São Paulo bookstores, entire shelves are stocked with writings about "Umbandismo," occultism, "white and black magic," spiritualism, astrology in respect to Umbanda, etc.[105] These books are a symptom of the attempt by the Luso-Brazilian world to comprehend Umbanda. They have actually had a retroactive effect on Umbanda over time.[106]

The concept Umbanda has its origins in Angola, where is it widespread in the southern two-thirds and the eastern half of the country. *Umbanda* in Kimbundu and Umbundu, as well as in numerous other languages (*vumbanda* in Ngangela, etc.) simply means knowledge and practice of the art of healing. *Kimbanda* (in the Kimbundu language), *ocimbanda* (in Umbundu), and *cimbanda* (in Ngangela) is a person who practices this indigenous medicine.

The area of origin and core range of this concept appear to lie in language zone R (according to Malcom Guthrie's division of Bantu languages), that, is, in the southwest part of Angola. It is here that the following pair of opposites appears in various languages' "magico-religious" terminology (Areia 1974): *ocimbanda* ("a traditional healer who also avails himself of means of divination") and *onganga* ("the sorcerer, the wizard/witch"). It is the task of the former to expose, neutralize and battle the machinations of the latter. His position in society is one of high regard.

Similar pairs of concepts also exist in Zone K. According to M.L. Rodrigues de Areia (1974), however, the distant northwest (the region corresponding to the former Kingdom of Kôngo, in the language zone H) uses another terminology which does not include the word *umbanda*. The region of the former Kingdom of Kôngo can therewith be excluded as possible zone of origin for Brazilian umbanda practices.

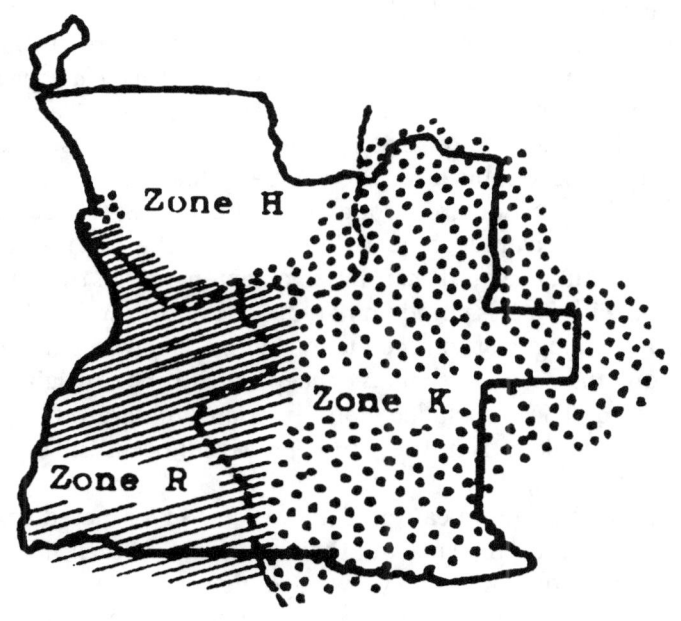

Core and dispersion zones of the concept umbanda in Angola
(map adapted from M.L. Rodrigues de Areia 1974, 2)

Among the duties of an *ocimbanda* or *kimbanda* in Angola is the symbolic communication with unsatisfied transcendental beings that would be likely to inflict a disease on a living person.

This contact is only possible via a professional medium, whose body serves as a vessel for the invoked "spirit," and who in this way is capable of serving as the speech and motion mechanism enabling communication with people (that is, to connect with humans). The "spirit" speaks through the medium to the gathered listeners, and is identified through the vastly changed, distorted voice of the medium. I had several opportunities to document entire sessions for the so-called *mahamba* (illness-inducing spirits) amongst the East Angolan people in southeast Angola (1965) and the northwest Zambian border area (1971). This material includes sound recordings, film, photos and notes and is as yet unpublished.[107]

These practices found a seamless continuation in Brazil. Southwest Angolan medical science was exported through transatlantic slaving to Brazil and is still known there today, albeit with many modifications, as *umbanda*. At first *umbanda* appeared to be prevalent only in the area of the the state of São Paulo. Originally it was also regarded in the south of Brazil as a purely Angolan tradition, but over the course of many decades it was vastly influenced due to strong cultural contacts between populations of African descent within Brazil. In the twentieth century the influence of African-Brazilian extensions of the Yorùbá religion with its òrìṣà predominated. Òrìṣà figures were adopted into the catalogue of transcendental beings. Likewise, numerous religious and pseudo-religious concepts of European origin were integrated. These included non-Christian "underground" religious ideas taken from the European world: occultism, spiritualism, astrology, etc.

Brazilians of European descent were soon attracted to the practices of the Angolans and their progeny in Brazil. The doctrines of Angolan medical knowledge, however, are based on a different perception of the world than that of the Europeans, and are also grounded in different ideas about human nature. As a result there were gaps in comprehension from the very start on the part of the Luso-Brazilians observing these practices amongst their enslaved Africans in Brazil for the first time. These comprehension gaps make themselves apparent in numerous cases described in the ethnological literature. As always, when someone is confronted with an unfamiliar cultural phenomenon, he or she tries to comprehend it in the framework of their own conceptual world. Umbanda was described with concepts like "religion," "cult," also occasionally "sorcery" and "magic." Adherents of European underground religions who had come to Brazil as immigrants from the Old World soon began to occupy themselves with Umbanda. They projected their own ideas onto these practices of the Angolan descendants and even founded their own Umbanda clubs. Angolan terminology, aligning itself to the stereotypes of the Luso-Brazilian world as well as European and West African symbolism, was in part also soon altered. For example, the word Umbanda in Brazil today means "good" white magic (*magia branca*), while the word *kimbanda* (which in Angola means a person practicing Umbanda) means "evil" black magic (*magia negra*). In Brazilian orthography the word is written "quimbanda." The picture is even more complicated by the fact that racist preconceptions were also passed on within this antagonistic black-white symbolism.

In the following table we show an overview of how Angolan concepts changed in the setting of Brazil:

Time ⟶

in Angola (*southern and eastern parts*)	*in Brazil*
Umbanda = traditional medicine, traditional healing practices through invocation and with support of transcendental beings (*mahamba*, etc.) via a medium	Umbanda = 1. A religion whose core is the contact with transcendental beings via a medium; 2. "magia branca" (healing good magic within the religious framework)
Kimbanda = traditional healing practitioner; doctor (also *ocimbanda*)	"Quimbanda" = "magia negra" (black magic, evil sorcery that kills and annihilates)

The continued usage in Brazil of both these originally Angolan concepts, *umbanda* and *kimbanda*, but with changed meanings (and actually as polarized concepts) requires an explanation. Semantic changes of this kind do not just sprout up by accident, but rather come into being due to certain needs. They have meaning and a function.

Why did not the concept *vwanga* or *wanga* for "evil magic" continue to be used in Brazil since it was connected with this meaning in broad areas of Angola and southern Congo? Why was the concept *kimbanda*, which had absolutely nothing to do with "evil magic," stigmatized? The answer to these questions can only be sought in an examination of the social relationships in colonial Brazil.

We heard that *umbanda* in Angola is a highly regarded institution providing treatment and healing of psychiatric and somatic illnesses and problems. What exactly is meant by *umbanda* in Brazil? What changed there?

At this point it is crucial to look at content and people: today the members and followers of *umbanda* are to a great extent Euro-Brazilians, who are perhaps even in the majority. Following the repression of the *kimbanda* figure the institution became increasingly "white." I particularly got the impression in 1979 in São Paulo that Umbanda is considered a growing phenomenon, albeit as a religious manifestation of an ever increasing number of ethnic non-Africans. This impression is confirmed by more recent Brazilian publications about Umbanda (e.g. Ortiz 1978; Pereira de Queiroz 1981). In large cities Umbanda frequently functions as a kind of alternative religion, a tank for collection of all those ideas that on the one hand don't fit into official Catholicism and on the other do not correspond to "modern" materialist world views. This form of Umbanda has very little left in common with *umbanda* in Angola. Certainly it comes as no surprise that in Brazil *umbanda* took on brand new functions little by little and adapted to the conditions of an urban Brazilian society in the country's industrial south.

One can speculate about why the word *kimbanda* (which in Angola is the term for the traditional healer) was completely reinterpreted on Brazilian soil and why, in the same pronunciation but different spelling "quimbanda," it took on the meaning *magia negra* ("black magic"). The negative reinterpretation of this Angolan concept for the person who was the healer is connected without doubt to the cultural clash of value concepts of the ruling Euro-Brazilian classes with those of subservient African descendants. From their perspective, the person, and not the knowledge, would have had the greater visibility. Thus it was the person, as originator of the repudiated practices, that became the object of attack, as well as the confusion between harmful and protective magic (as in the practices of a *kimbanda*) as still crops up even in today's (European language) publications. In European languages the general concept "magic" (Portuguese: *magia*) refers to both practices.

In Angola there is no comparable pair of concepts. The "evil magic" is called, for example, *vulozi*, elsewhere *vwanga* or *wanga*. It is not burdened with black/white magic at all. "Good magic" does not exist; therefore there is no concept opposite to "evil magic." Add to this the fact that the general concept "medicines" (like *vihemba* in the Ngangela languages of East Angola) comprises both those that are used to heal (*kusaka*) and those that "enchant" or "kill through enchantment" (*kuloza*).

The figure of the "black healer" (*kimbanda*) began to be regarded more and more negatively due to the influence of Christian religions on the one hand, and through self-abasement of the African people due to their status as enslaved individuals on the other. The "black healer" was associated with the sharing of medicines that were decried by the Luso-Brazilians as "dark," "heathen" practices.

In the next developmental phase of these transformations of meaning, it must have happened that the progeny of the enslaved Africans from Angola in Brazil identified themselves with outsiders' assessment of their traditional healing practices' representatives. At the same time, however, the need to continue the *umbanda* healing practices could not be eliminated because the Old World had huge deficiencies in the area of psychosomatics, and was unable to replace what Angolan medicine offered. Therefore *Umbanda* survived as a healing practice with a background in Angolan religious concepts; and so did, naturally, the figure of the healer, but no longer with the name *kimbanda*.

In the south of Brazil, as African languages were just being forgotten on a broad scale, a peculiar double-think mindset was developing amongst Angolan descendants. The figure of the *kimbanda* (which had become a symbol for the African ego of the oppressed) was eliminated, the subject itself however, *umbanda*—

indispensable in the enslaved community—was idealized in the sense of the enslaved African man's attempted self-redemption from the despised image of "sorcerer" or "black magic" practitioner.

During colonial times the religious practices in Africa were no less subject to enormous pressure. This also rubbed off on the terminology there; for instance even today in French-speaking West Africa, traditional healers are called "charlatans," and this expression is also used by other local Africans. A total denigration of traditional healers in Africa could not have taken place, however, because the colonial period was much too short, and in the meantime indigenous medicine has been recognized worldwide, including the World Health Organization. In colonial Brazil, on the other hand, there was no recourse of this kind. The Angolan descendants in the south of the country identified themselves more and more with the negative value judgements by others and relegated the figure of their own nation's healers to the unconscious, beginning to equate the healer from the perspective of the Luso-Brazilians with an "evil sorcerer." The concept of "quimbanda" developed from this. Because, however, the belief in healing powers of a traditional African healer could not be totally extinguished, the *idea of the person* itself was extracted from the concept "quimbanda" and transferred to the figure of "pai-de-santo" in Umbanda.

The depersonalized concept "quimbanda" remained and represented from then on "evil magic" of an African coloring as expressed by *vulozi, vwanga, ufiti* (Cinyanja), *uchawi* (Kiswahili) or other words in various Bantu languages.

What was retained, therefore, was a favorable image of the African healing practice, but divorced from its practitioners! *Umbanda* as healing practice became disassociated from the *kimbanda*, the healer, his or her skin color being equated with sorcey or "black magic" (*magia negra*). This was the new meaning, expressed in the (depersonalized) concept "quimbanda." A polarization resulted, a dichotomy of good versus evil. *Umbanda* became the good "white magic" (*magia branca*).

In summary, it can be said that the changes which *umbanda* underwent on Brazilian soil were incisive. The characteristics of Umbanda in Brazil—which are not common to those of *umbanda* in Angola—are primarily as follows:

1. The increasing polarization of the universe into "good" and "evil," good and bad powers.

2. The infliction of unconscious racist ideas on the concepts "black" and "white"; and in this context the use of the word "magia" in a manner that had no equivalent in Bantu languages, specifically, interchangeable positive and negative auguries (attributes) whereby "black" was perceived as negative and "white" as positive.

3. The change in social and religious function from the Angolan one.

However, there are still elements common to both Umbanda in Brazil and *umbanda* in Angola, including, amongst others:

1. The ambition and intention to heal, particularly to relieve people of psychological problems and suffering.

2. Creation of a harmony with transcendental beings. Humans must recognize their intentions and possible dissatisfaction and act accordingly.

3. Contact with the beings of the transcendental world is forged with the help of a medium.

4. Initiation rites are conducted for anyone aspiring to become a medium and an inner circle of members.

5. Although followers of Umbanda are unaware of it, many key words in Angolan languages are still found in Brazilian Umbanda today; for example, the word "pemba," derived from common words in numerous Angolan languages, such as *pemba*, *mpemba* or *mphemba*, meaning white kaolin or white chalk. This is a substance with significant symbolic value in Angolan cultures (cf. Kubik 1982) and it has been kept in Brazilian Umbanda ceremonies. "Pemba" and others are used in the "cruzamento" ceremony of a new medium.

Decoration of boats in Salvador/Bahia with "orixá" figures: "Oxum," "Oxala," "Iêmanja" or "Janaina," etc. October 1975. Photos by G. Kubik.

Nagô/Yorùbá Candomblé event in Salvador/Bahia, 20 October 1974. Drawn by Descartes Gadelha.

The drum ensemble of the Candomblé, 20 October 1974. Drawn by Descartes Gadelha.

Umbanda in southwest Angola: Divinator and indigenous healer (kimbanda) Emilia Kakinda (female), about 40 years old. Location: Quicuco (Kikuku), region of Dinde/ Quilengues, Provincia de Wila (Huíla), Angola, July 1965. Photos by G. Kubik (F 74).

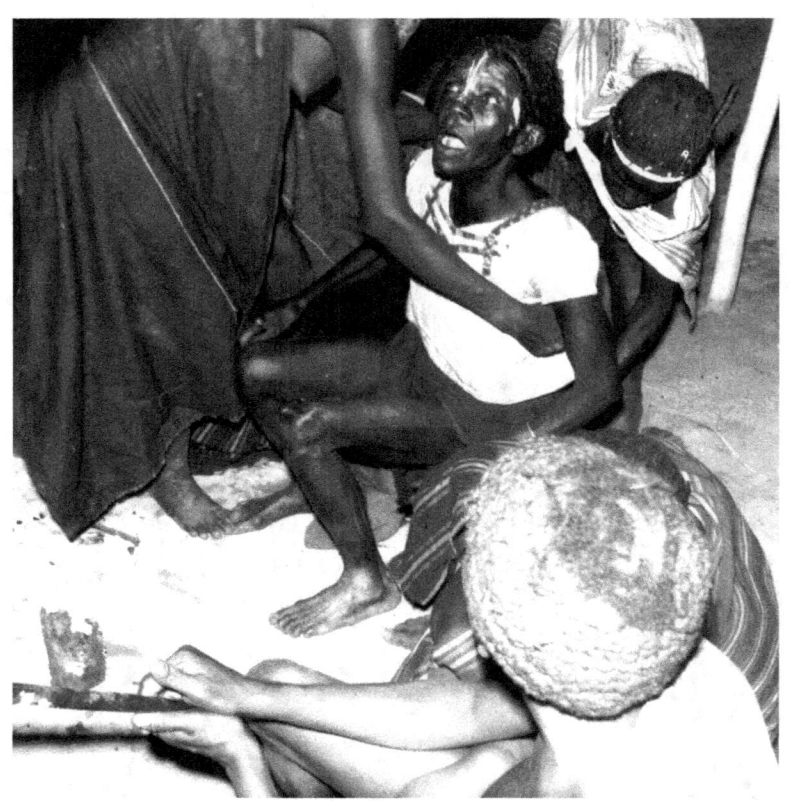

*A medium in a trance and the use of mphemba in East Angola.
a) Nya Vungamba, the mother of Sankhenga (the husband of the
sick woman) is possessed by a discontent transcendental being
(lihamba) and speaks with its voice to those gathered around.*

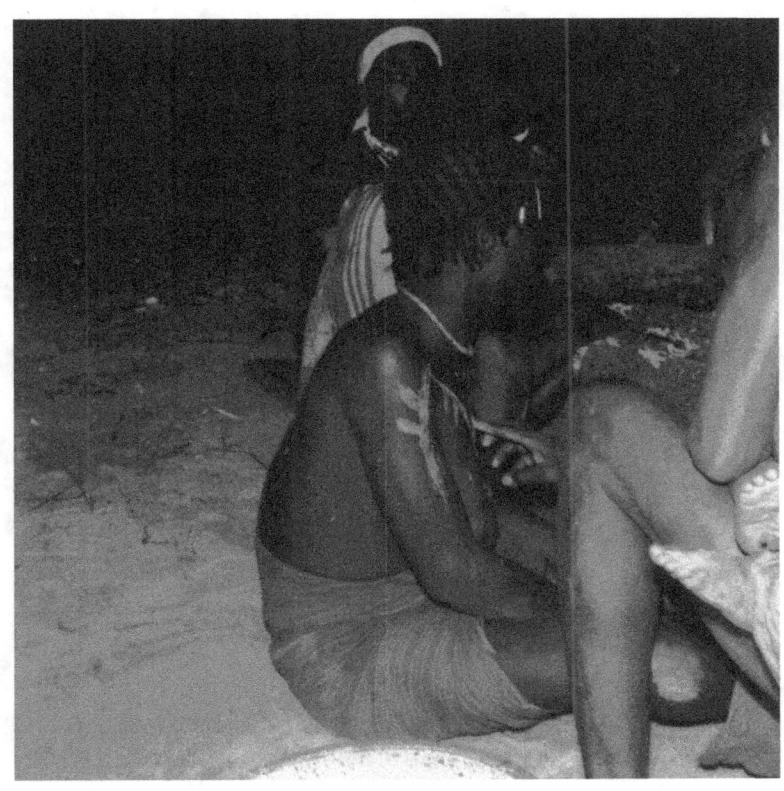

b) White kaolin (mphemba) is used to paint the sick woman. Village: Sachingangu in the region of Chisende, Circunscrição de Longa, Provincia Kwandu-Kuvangu, Angola, December 1965. Photos by G. Kubik.

Umbanda in Brazil: two photos.
a) View of the entrance to the temple of the "Tenda Espiritual de Umbanda, Justiça de Xangô," São Paulo, 12 May 1979. Photo by G. Kubik (No. 15/37).

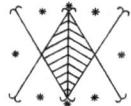

ON THE METHODOLOGY OF AFRICAN-BRAZILIAN CULTURAL RESEARCH

Our area of research comprises the study of all cultural manifestations, including those of verbal communication in the sense of sociolinguistics, amongst representatives of African-Brazilian cultures both past and present. Constituents of African-Brazilian cultures are defined as people who have plainly been determined by African cultural heritage in their overall behavior, conceptions and knowledge, regardless of their physical-anthropological differences. It must be emphasized that a representative of African-Brazilian cultural traits is not identifiable by appearance (e.g. skin color), although the vast majority do carry physically dominant or—at least—immediately discernable features of African ancestry.

In Brazil the current relationships between cultures and their correlations with socio-economic conditions are being studied. In addition, a broad range of research is being dedicated to reconstruction of the history of African cultures on Brazilian soil with the support of written, illustrative and oral sources, archaeological artefacts, and other evidence examined in chronological sequence.

Herskovits's vocabulary of "retentions," "survivals," "selection" and "reinterpretation" is no longer sufficient for this area of research (although these terms are still significant concepts in African diaspora studies). Above all, the concept of "acculturation" has been criticized from various sides, also by African colleagues. By now it is evident that various African cultural traits in Brazil and elsewhere in the Americas are not simply retentions as part of an all-encompassing panorama of acculturation, but rather it is so that intact African cultures in the form of neo-African extensions continue to survive in the Americas. It was for this reason that I suggested some years ago that we speak of African cultural *extensions* as we move forward in the field of African diaspora studies.[108] This positive formulation of the African presence in the Americas has in the meantime been endorsed by many of my colleagues.

African cultures are present in the Americas in one way in the form of geographically limited cultural niches; in another way as primarily urban forms of mutation and assimilation displaying predominantly African character. African cultural niches and zones continue to survive in Brazil in the same way that specific European cultures do (e.g. the case of a German cultural extension in the city of Blumenau in state of Santa Catarina). We assume that no one-sided acculturation to European cultures took place in the Americas, but rather that all cultures, retaining some inherent elements of their ethnicities, assimilated attractive elements from the contact cultures with no loss to their own integrity. This *can* lead to total amalgamation at an advanced stage of cultural contact, at which point the original cultures vanish. However, due to the social conditions in the Americas this more intense cultural merger rarely occurred on a broad scale.

In regard to interactions between various cultures in *cultural contact*, there are basically two separate defined processes, which in many cases advance independently over long periods of time. In terms of cultural expression, or, in an analogy to linguistics, processes take place in the "cultural" vocabulary of a group in a similar way to those taking place in language.[109] The two processes diverge in opposite directions:

1. The retention of an indigenous "language" (one's own culturally specific vocabulary and concepts in a more or less comprehensive scope, including certain manifestations of reduction, blending and modification).

2. The imitation of the foreign "language" (the foreign culture-specific vocabulary with implied concepts), which, however, due to projection of the indigenous culture, is actually a creolization.

The point of departure is different for the two developments resulting from culture contact. In the first process, the culture learned early retains its framework of values within the perception of self; however, foreign cultural borrowings are inserted into it. In the second process, an external devaluation of a group's own culture makes it impossible to try to retain it, and the group *wants* to comprehensively adopt the foreign culture (more precisely, that of the oppressor). Thus the group aspires to undergo a total and unconditional acculturation, at least on the surface. This cannot succeed, however; first due to the difficulties of the adaptation, similar to that of learning a foreign language; and secondly due to unconscious resistance, so it is bound to fail.

Once initiated, the two processes can achieve various levels of manifestation. In both process 1 and process 2 something new develops as a result. Process 1 enriches and transforms the indigenous "cultural language" through diverse "stylish" cultural borrowings; however, the basic structure is retained, and the "language" receives some fresh make-up. In process 2, the foreign culture is reinterpreted unconsciously from the angle of a remembered cultural heritage, and is then reconfigured so as to become manageable. Something new results in the sense of a cultural creolization. In process 1 an indigenous idiom is retained and continues to serve as a basis of the cultural system, while also being influenced and modified by various external influences. In process 2, a foreign tradition is adopted, emulated and changed very quickly to the extent that the result must be something completely new.

It is also important to differentiate whether single elements from a foreign culture are being adopted as "decorative" additions to the indigenous one (like borrowings of isolated foreign language expressions), or if large, systematically associated parts (or even the entire system) are adopted and then reinterpreted within the perspective of the still active indigenous culture. In the first case the foreign elements are only cosmetic, and in the second case conscious "acculturation" results, while unconsciously there is usually a simultaneous rejection of the foreign culture. This leads to multiple forms of conflicting behavior and to symptoms of compensation which often appear many generations later. The two processes can also continue symbiotically, or process 1 may be succeeded by process 2 in a later epoch.

In contrast to the complex relationships outlined above, the concept of acculturation springs from a linear model of cultural contact and thus from the implied thought that on our planet there may be "advanced" and "more highly developed" cultures to which the "weaker," "less developed" or "underdeveloped" ones should conform. Pseudo-historic models with an evolutionary structure (like the assumption of universally valid stages in a unilinear cultural development of humankind) have up to now enriched cultural and social researchers only with ideologies. These models have not led to a realistic assessment of the forces of history based on facts. As has been observed, such models have mostly served to advance one or another form of cultural or political imperialism.

Cultures can arguably adopt an offensive or defensive character in certain historical time periods. Over the course of time this can be reversed. For example, Islamic culture was sometimes on the offensive, sometimes on the defensive in various centuries and regions. Cultures on the offensive claim cultural superiority in one or another form. In various epochs and areas of the world these claims are verbalized in various ways. In one historical period a certain culture can, for example, frame its claim through a "ranking model" through which it characterizes its own and some other cultures deemed to be closely related as "high culture." Accordingly, a contrasting category, such as "primitive cultures," is generated. It then becomes the task of scholars within this closed system to formulate criteria justifying this ideological pretension, such as the presence or absence of selected cultural traits like an alphabetic script, or a specific technology, etc. This claim to superiority by a culture on the offensive took other guises in earlier epochs; for example, by employing categories like "modernity" or "progressiveness," or by making a claim of "first world" status (projecting a ruling-class image on a large scale) in contrast to a "second," "third" or even "fourth" and "fifth" world (projecting a lower-class image on a large scale).

During the formation of such historical configurations, the reactions from the side of those cultures forced into a defensive position were ample. The result was anything but a docile, one-direction cultural adaptation (acculturation) perceived as "emancipation" from the colonizing culture's perspective. Just the opposite: one of the most important reactions is a symbolic *ingestion* of the culture on the offense by adherents to the culture on the defense via a detour by identifying with the oppressor. This is not "adaptation"; rather it includes the annihilation of the oppressor.

Encounters of cultures espousing different norms and demands can lead to very diverse and not necessarily predictable results. They can only be historically documented case by case. Sometimes the result is a sort of *transculturation* (a concept of Fernando Ortiz 1940; see also Kubik 1979b). In other cases the culture on the defense infiltrates the one claiming superiority on a subliminal basis and "infects" those members, therewith catapulting itself into an offensive position. This scenario exists often in Brazil. Africa strongly affects the behavior and thinking of Brazilians of European ancestry on an unconscious level—as can be shown many times over. Fernando A. A. Mourão seems to hint at something similar when he wrote:

> As 'white' men began to frequent the 'terreiros' and were brought up in households with a 'black' nanny, they began to internalize elements (from the other side) that would converge to create a new mentality. This is also the case of Africans who in part are faithful to principles of awareness of a power that involves everything, but in some cases already in part individualized. In that situation he will solicit benefits, not as a consequence of action perceived as a coherent whole, but as a veritable grace obtained through the practice of rites in whose context the myth got lost or had changed its meaning. It is at that point—depending on the extent to which structural continuity was interrupted and the person in society became a mirror of the new situation—that a synthesis emerged.[110]

As already set out in this book's introduction, the concept of "roots" is unsuitable as a theoretical term for examination of the history of African cultures in the Americas. "Roots" became fashionable again in the seventies thanks to the global success of the book of the same name by Alex Haley (1977) and the TV series with LeVar Burton as Kunta Kinte.[111] As in many areas of the humanities, in this case linguistics, where one speaks of the root of a word and word stems, the model of a tree (with trunk, roots and branches) played a large role in the efforts of Europeans and Euro-Americans researching the African diaspora cultural scene in the Americas. A systematic review of documents shows the use of such words in astounding frequency. In the meantime African history research is being promoted at countless African and non-African universities. As a result the historical connections between Africa and Afro-America have been reconstructed through detailed source analysis.

The prevailing tendencies surrounding African-Brazilian cultures in somewhat older literature may be outlined as follows. First, ideas about Africa as a "dark" continent "without a history" persisted and still persist, even in Africa. Perceptions of Africa as a site of stagnant cultural traditions, thrown into motion only through European colonization, still exist today. Second, in connection with this, there is a predominance of panoramic perspectives towards Africa on the part of both numerous Brazilian and American authors in general. Regarded from the perspective on the other side of the Atlantic, Africa often appears to be a uniform bloc. The African segment of African diaspora history was not only treated ahistorically, but also seen from an American viewpoint in a relatively undifferentiated way. Many cultural elements and complexes that were exported from Africa to the Americas were simply described as "West African" without exploring their history based on source material from Africa in addition to that from the Americas. Third, only a few Brazilian cultural researchers (or those specializing in Brazil) had field experience in both African-Brazilian and African cultures. This shortcoming was particularly noticeable in the area of Bantu cultures and somewhat less in the area of West Africa, where the leading researchers (like Arthur Ramos, Roger Bastide and Pierre Verger) were undertaking field work on both sides of the Atlantic. This situation explains the conspicuous persistence, for almost half a century, of one Brazilian author after another relying on the same, relatively minimal data on Africa that was available at the time. Fourth, a general inclination still exists in the Brazilian national consciousness to disparage African elements in favor of overall Brazilian culture. This is an inherited psychological holdover from the colonial past. Even the African background of the African-Brazilian *folguedos* like the "Congada" is occasionally denied. The mass media systematically present Brazil as "white." It may seem a trivial example that there is a predilection to crown a blond, white Brazilian woman "Miss Brazil" in a beauty contest, but this is symptomatic. In the Brazilian mass media, black cultures are almost uniformly presented as "vestiges" or disappearing residual manifestations and conceptualized from the point of view of a Euro-Brazilian culture that regards itself as superior. This reflects the massive psychological repression of everything stemming from the realm of former enslaved Africans and their progeny. The black political movement in Brazil (*Movimento Negro Unificado*) attributed this situation to a political motivation: "white rulership" must be maintained. Brazil cannot be allowed to come under suspicion of not being a "white country." A few years ago the *Movimento Negro* demanded the reintroduction of the question of racial affiliation in the national census. The reason for the original ban by the government was not to promote a multi-racial society, but rather to make the appearance of the actual number of Africans as small as possible.[112] If an author like the cultural and social scientist Kazadi wa Mukuna, born in Congo and educated at the University of São Paulo, steps forward and holds up a cultural mirror to Brazilians (cf. Kazadi 1979), he is in danger of being accused of black racism. Fifth, a widely prevalent stereotype in African-Brazilian (and, in general, the African diaspora) literature is the opinion that African cultural elements in the Americas have become so blended and "acculturated" in the meantime that they can no longer be singularly traced to precise regions in Africa. It is often maintained that it is now impossible to specify exact African regions of origin for single African-Brazilian cultural traits or complexes. Lastly, in those areas where a regional assignment cannot be ignored because it is so obvious, there was a tendency to overemphasize the West African and underemphasize and neglect the Bantu portion of Brazil's composite cultural panorama. Fernando A.A. Mourão (1980, 5) attributes this to a widespread opinion amongst Brazilians and numerous foreign authors that

West Africans, in particular the Yorùbá with their òrìṣà cosmology, represent a "higher culture" than do Bantu Africans. In this way concepts of "stages" and "levels" of cultural development prejudice the direction and content of research projects. Mourão writes (1980, 1) in regard to the recent bibliographies on African cultural influences in Brazil:

> Recent bibliographical lists concerned with African influences in Brazil attract once more our attention to the fact that Sudanic Africa is being systematically privileged to the detriment of Bantu Africa, both as it concerns the number of works published and the degree of their profundity.[113]

Mourão writes (1980, 7-8) with special reference to the bibliography of Cristina Argenton Colonelli (1971):

> While studies about blacks of Sudanic origin are present at all levels, with rare exceptions, works about the Bantu are usually limited to studies of folklore, and even here among the 3,188 bibliographical items we have only identified about 30 dealing with folklore of Bantu origin in a more specific manner.[114]

Mourão has devoted himself for some years to changing this situation. Apart from his own journeys to Angola (he is author of a book on modern Luso-Angolan literature, Mourão 1978), he managed to attract eminent African specialists to the university and his Centro de Estudos Africanos, which also publishes a journal, África. On his staff in 1975 were Kazadi wa Mukuna and Kabengele Munanga from the Congo and Carlos Moreira Henrique Serrano from Cabinda (R.P. Angola). Invited foreign guest professors in 1974-75 included important researchers like Cheick Anta Diop of IFAN, Dakar, as well as scholars from the Congo, Ivory Coast, Dahomey (Benin), Zambia and Senegal.

Given the relationships described here, three approaches are recommended for cultural investigation procedures in the area of Brazil as well as most other parts of the Americas. The following should be carried out concurrently and parallel to each other:

(a) Analysis of historic sources from both African diaspora and the African-area cultural worlds to which cultural contacts existed, and a systematic comparison in the framework of ethnohistorical methodology (cf. Hirschberg 1966, Sturtevant 1966 et al).

(b) Comparison of data from the contemporary Afro-Americas with those from modern-day Black Africa – from an African perspective and with methods developed in Africa.

(c) Interpretation of current data originating in one of the two areas using historical sources from the other, as well as interpretation of historical data from both areas in light of current data.

An important goal of such investigation is two-fold: reconstruction of historical processes in the cultural area on the one hand, as well as the exploration of causes and rationale underpinning selective processes and cultural transformations. In other words, why did African-Brazilians retain certain traits, or process them into new configurations, from certain cultural regions of Africa? Why did they give up others completely?

For ethnohistorians, point (a) requires no further discussion. However, points (b) and (c)—comparison of current material from both areas and comparison over the course of history using interpretations across time distance—presents a methodological problem. This issue can be summed up in a question: Is it possible to prove, using non-historical methods, that certain cultures did retain stability in some specific elements, if not as a whole? African cultures in two parts of the world separated by the vast expanse of an ocean would inevitably develop in different directions over the time-span of centuries. They were each absorbing influences from other cultures as well (European and to some extent Amerindian, especially in South America). Given this complex background, are we still able to reconstruct the main directions of culture-historical changes from the tiny sample of contemporary expressions we have from the 1970s and 1980s?

Yes, we can—both where cultures have changed and in the areas where they have remained stable or for the most part identical on both sides. It would follow that such a comparison based on material evidence, conceptual and structural identity, is legitimate. If a culture becomes divided through geographic separation of its population and the resultant daughter cultures develop so divergently that they are no longer recognizable, then in that state they are no longer comparable. In our area of research, however, this is never the case. A large proportion of the African diaspora were only abducted from Africa during the eighteenth and nineteenth century. Three to four hundred years is much too short a time period to allow for complete divergence. This is evident in the area of linguistics: Portuguese is still spoken in Brazil. Divergence in the twentieth century between the Brazilian forms of Portuguese and those of Portugal, Angola, Mozambique, São Tomé, and Guinea-Bissau has not yet reached a level where it would be possible to regard Brazilian as an independent language. Similar to the relative slow developmental divergence in languages, the advancement of mutations and amalgamations of various transplanted African cultures in Brazil has not yet reached that point where any of those cultures could no longer be identified.

It is also certain that singular aspects of a culture can change at various rates. The speed of changes within a culture is therefore neither constant nor concurrent. Some cultural elements are even prone to exhibit an extraordinarily historical sluggishness. This could, for example, be the case where a cultural feature is accorded a particularly central function within the cultural entity or complex.[115]

A completely new area of investigation comes to the fore with the conjecture that unconscious processes can play a role in the passing down of culture traits. I demonstrated this in 1979 with Brazilian examples (Kubik 1979a, 49-51). In summary, the following can be asserted: a cultural feature can temporarily disappear from the surface (of perceptible manifestations) of a certain culture for perhaps fifty or a hundred years. Verbal references to it may also be gone. After a while, however, if conditions are favorable—molded by, for example, radical social change or a crisis situation like war—the culture traits which was lost suddenly gets "reinvented."

In reality something was being constantly passed down the whole time. As it were, under the perceptible surface, probably a syndrome of interrelational behavioral patterns that contain the "lost" culture traits in condensed form (like on microfilm) as a *possibility*. Whatever gets passed on in such cases is not a certain conscious knowledge of a cultural feature, but rather an abstract "programming" enabling an effortless "reinvention" at a favorable point in time. The carriers of such programming are unaware of this and of the processes involved.

A tradition, for example friction-based fire-making or techniques of iron ore mining, can completely disappear from the manifest phenomenology of a culture (when, for example, other techniques for fire-starting or ore mining have been borrowed). Nevertheless, the intracultural experiences do not become fully obsolete straight away. They are still passed down *unconsciously* through related learning over a longer period, perhaps two or three generations, even if they no longer have a manifest form of appearance within the culture. The knowledge of friction fire-making is then not passed down as an image, but rather as an abstract code, or a readiness of behavior which can lead to a "reinvention" in certain situations within the context of culture traits linked to fire-making forming a network of ideas.

The transfer takes place through various verbal and non-verbal interactions between people of the particular culture—people who have no apparent connection to the lost tradition. In fact, the obsolete cultural knowledge is never directly verbalized. What is passed on is a disposition to reinvention, actually more of a repeat journey along a path already traveled. It may have been a long time since this path was last traveled, and as a result it may be psychologically full of tangles; however, it still presents an opportunity and, when conditions demand, it can suddenly be traveled anew. On that note, for example, in Brazil the playing method of a *lamellophone* (a common musical instrument in Central Africa, cf. Kubik 1979a, 1986a) includes a choice: it can be done with the thumbs or forefingers—pointing to two different African playing traditions—even though lamellophones are no longer found in Brazil today.

In a similar way, it appears that Maculelê still contains a cultural memory of Angolan boys' initiation schools even though the central element, the circumcision surgery, has vanished and was even suppressed in Brazil. It is also characteristic that a definitive set of behavioral patterns (e.g. the attitude and manner of striking the sticks) was passed on, though non-verbally. In all such cases the behavorial set can lead to reconstruction and re-constitution of the "lost trait"—the actual trait which has long been forgotten. This is what I term *unconscious transmission of culture traits*; unconscious because the carriers of the traits in question are no longer aware of its meaning, and therefore cannot be directly asked in an interview to explain it.

Following the disappearance of a cultural trait, a sort of code may thus be conveyed through future generations. This code is an *abstract expression* of the feature within a larger context of different culture-producing codes. It is passed along through human interaction within the process of enculturation. The lost culture trait continues to exist as a latent component (in an abstract encryption) of this code.

Unconscious transmittal is conducive to biological survival. It forms a reserve of culturally learned material to fall back upon in an emergency, for example, in a crisis situation (war, etc.).

Traditions can be repressed in a cultural group due to an aggressive social environment. During times of slavery and oppression it is possible that the ruling culture violently silences a group's specific cultural characteristics. These features do not actually become extinct; they retreat into a more secure area of the human psyche. All external manifestations of these cultural characteristics are indeed forgotten. However, something like a replica remains and is stamped into the unconscious. It becomes a component of a behavioural set. The "lost" element is then transferred unwittingly from parents to children, from one generation to the next, through behavioral patterns associated with the set, or through "related" cultural characteristics. After two or three generations someone suddenly invents something without knowing that his ancestors already traveled down the same path. Take, for example, the case of an eighteenth century enslaved African community in which drums were forbidden. The drums were burned; and it is possible that all drums actually vanished and were never played again. The drumming rhythm patterns, however, lived on—in a *mute* coding. They still exist as a form of movement, as a system of kinetic behavior. They are handed down from one generation to the next in this coded form, without words, through non-verbal communication. In another century they suddenly resurface, maybe on drums, maybe in another form.

This implies that in the Americas there is much more African heritage buried beneath the surface and stored on cultural "microfilm" than one might think. The presence of such traditions or behavioral dispositions—which may be totally unconscious—can be tracked in several ways. One is the use of a so-called "cultural comprehension test" (cf. Kubik 1979a, 50-51). The test subject is shown cultural material, like an object or symbolic action, or a certain behavior, and careful observations are made to determine whether the reaction elicited in the subject demonstrates comprehension or incomprehension. It is possible, after a larger number of separate tests over a period of time, to delineate a cultural profile of the subject. The theoretical underpinnings are that subliminal awareness can be reactivated by cultural material from the region of the world corresponding to the person's cultural (not necessarily genetic) descendant. The person reacts with either "known" (comprehend; positive reaction) or "unknown" (incomprehension; negative, indifferent reaction). If the person is a carrier of an area's tradition which has since become obsolete but lingers on below the surface, there will be a positive reaction. There are no ambiguous reactions, only positive or negative (although in the case of complex material it is possible that various single components yield different results).

An "ethical" issue does, however, arise because the test subject cannot be told that he/she is in a test situation, otherwise the results may be skewed. For this reason such tests are best done in the framework of random social contact. A verbal introduction can be made (or not) as desired. In the former case, the following words could precede the test: "I have something here that I'd like to show you," whereby the object is shown or the action carried out. In the second case, there is no introduction. If it is an object being examined, it is simply placed so that the test subject will see it. If it is a visual or auditory event being examined, it should be carried out at an appropriate time when the test subject is as relaxed as possible. All *spontaneous* reactions, whether verbal or non-verbal, are assessed; as far as possible, no questions should be asked.

In the framework of a restructuring of the methodology of African diaspora studies, the involvement of African colleagues in African diaspora research projects is particularly important. Quite simply, this can be of experimental value in field research. Due to a different cultural background many African observers react to the African diaspora scene in the Americas in a way somewhat different from European observers, no matter how specialized the latter may be in the study of African cultures. Often the African researcher makes observations that would completely evade European or Brazilian researchers. I tested this out in 1974 when I visited South America for the very first time with an African associate. Africans working in artistic professions seem to have a particularly good chance of discovering something new since they often have a higher cultural sensitivity. On the other hand, the reaction of the African diaspora population to an African field researcher or a mixed African/European team seemed—at least in Brazil—to be very positive, as has been observed in the experiences of Kazadi wa Mukuna and our own experiences in 1974 (with Donald Kachamba) and 1980 (with Donald Kachamba and Moya A. Malamusi). Our 1974 stay in Venezuela was too short to arrive at any conclusive findings and I do not have reliable data so far from the USA. But the majority of African-Brazilians we contacted grappled psychologically with African visitors in one way or another. This often went to a point of intensively projecting unconscious expectations. Our experience, particularly during lengthier studies in Brazil, was that an African visitor was usually perceived as a representative of the "lost African self." In many cases transference, in a psychoanalytical sense, develops, allowing emotional attitudes developed by the African-Brazilian (depending on his own personal background) in relation to his "African soul" to surface. If this "soul" has been repressed from consciousness and relegated to a stunted existence, it means that this person has internalized normative concepts of "white" culture to an excessive degree. Accordingly, the first encounter with Africans will be cool and sceptical. However, in an odd way many African-Brazilians are fascinated by African visitors despite linguistic communication difficulties. In one or another form an internal realignment takes place. In many cases the African-Brazilian's sudden tangible enlightenment is a first-time self-awareness of his own unknown, impenetrable psychological layers.

Thus the African visitor digs deep under the skin, to the inner layers, of the African-Brazilian merely through his or her presence and the resulting human contacts in a field situation. These layers were previously sealed and shut away. Critical situations, as well as psychologically cathartic ones, can develop—and long forgotten memories and behaviors resurface.

Questions posed by the African members of the research team are also especially revealing in that they (a) carry a certain fascination due to the African perspective, and lead to unexpected responses, or, on the other hand, (b) evoke typically emotionally-charged reactions from the African-Brazilians, allowing insights into the nature of the culturally imposed repression.

One of the two colleagues with whom I traveled in 1980, Moya A. Malamusi, asked the villagers of Cafundó three questions: (a) Whether there was any kind of *chinamwali* for the girls there? In Moya's home country, *chinamwali* is a process of traditional education following the onset of puberty. The answer was "No"; that was forbidden early on by the slaveholders. Implicit in this answer, however, is the idea that this concept—or at least the possibility of its existence—is still recalled today. (b) Whether the villagers buried their deceased themselves? Moya asked this question of the village head Otavio Caetano in the company of Sr. Noel Rosa de Almeida (approx. 40 years old) and other residents. They reacted with indignation to the question. They were visibly embarrassed when Moya related that this was a common practice back home. In this case Moya's question had hit a repressed inner layer. Alone the fact that he even asked such a question shows the high significance that the culture of his homeland assigns to the burial rites of the dead at the village cemetary. This was most likely also the case with the ancestors of the Cafundó residents. In the end they answered that they rejected this form of burial. Pedro, son of Silvino, married to a Luso-Brazilian woman, then added that, long ago, a dead person from Cafundó or Caxambu, whose body was tightly swathed, was carried on a litter by two men on foot to Salto de Pirapora, where he was buried in the cemetery. This place is about 15 kilometers away from Cafundó. All of Cafundó's dead are buried today in Salto de

Pirapora, he said. Sr. Sergio Coelho from Sorocaba told me later that the burial of the dead in the village is forbidden by a law documented in writing and archived at the Salto administration office. This African custom may have been forbidden very long ago, probably during the time of slavery. (c) A further question that Moya asked raised not one eyebrow. He wanted to know, how did one manage in this village of about just 40 residents to intermarry? The answer was that marriage between cousins did occur but that relatives had married quite a bit into the four former enslaved villages—Cafundó, Caxambu, Pilar do Sul and Fazendinha. Nowadays they also marry externally.

My own observations point to prevailing tendences among the younger generation to look for partners outside the community, mostly in the next town, Salto de Pirapora. As was also the case in past generations, the tendency of Cafundó's direct Angolan descendants leans in the direction of marrying "white" or at least finding a "light-skinned" partner.

APPENDIX

A. TEXT OF A CONVERSATION IN CAFUNDÓ VOCABULARY (EXCERPT)

Recording, tape A 63/II/4, of 13 April 1979 in Bairro do Cafundó, Municipio de Salto de Pirapora, the state of São Paulo. The recordings took place at the house of Ms. Valderez in Cafundó around 7 PM. Residents of neighboring houses as well as many children were present. After the village leader Otávio Caetano (male, around 60 years old) arrived, Ms. Maria de Lourdes Rosa de Almeida (about 35 years old) offered to recreate a dialogue in the "African language" with him.

In the following transcription from tape, the words from Angolan languages are italicized; Portuguese fill-words are in normal font. The numerous emotional reactions, laughing, exclamations, etc. which both participants masterfully wove into the text, gave it the character of a continuous conversation (although they did not necessarily refer to the contents) unfortunately could not be transcribed here.

It is clear to Cafundó residents that there is always a bit of fraud behind such conversations in the "African language," but this is a professional secret of the performers and it has sold well to visitors. The fact is that around 200 to 300 lexicographical items from various Angolan languages are still recalled today in Cafundó, and that from these one can create an impressive dialogue in "African" for (language illiterate) Luso-Brazilians.

Speakers:

O. = Otávio Caetano

L. = Maria de Lourdes Rosa de Almeida

Transcription and translation by G. Kubik

Text:

O. *Kwendâ no njo do turo do vimbundo.*
L. *Ààà! Jimbúndó ò*, mm, *tá kwenda no palule... onjo de sempre nani.*
O. *Aà! Cerio.* Mas que eu passo *kupopya* que e *kwendano do turo no vìmbundo*, que é...
L. *Aààl*
O. *Vavuro, do vìmbundo.*
L. *Oòò! no turo?*
O. *Èé!*
L. *No turo sempre sempre nani no jimbundo ò, o jìmbundo que e tá kwenda no pulule no turo.*
O. Mm.
L. *E tá perguntar nani.*
O. *Kupopya.*
L. *Kupopya.*
O. *Kupopya.*
L. *Nani né?*
O. *Kupopya nani. E pá kwenda mukándá à, ku mukândá vavuro, t'amhara vavuro, que é, que é nyamyanyara tá kusumbano.*
L. *Kusumbano, èè.*
O. *Èè nyamyanyara kusumbano.*
L. *A! Kupopya n'ambara vavuro?*
O. *Èè!*
L. *Nyamyanyará áà! Tá kusumbano*, sempre, pela então sempre *vavuro.*
O. *Vavuro.* Mas é ...
L. Mas sempre na sempre na... *kupopya nani?*
O. *Mmm nani, tá! Liii! Nguto o do injo kwenda n'onanga do muiombo pá pá konoako, ku japekava pá varya ku kapekavca.*
L. *Vavuro.*
O. *Vavuro.*
L. *Vavuro.* Bastante *vavuro no japekava.*
O. Certo. Porque ...
L. ... *tá kwendano.*
O. *Mbambi vavuro. Ombambi vavuro ... japekava, andaru!*
L. *Mambí, mambi andaru, andaru na tá nani!* Aá é assim.

APPENDIX

O.   *A á! Kwend'ovava. Kwend'ovava vavuro.*
L.   *Àá! Baba!*
O.   *Porque andaru kwenda daí na né?*
L.   (Laughing) *Aá na ondulo do nani o baba tem que ir vavuro. Vavuro no injo.*
O.   *E porque daí no konoa... Konoa.*
L.   *E e e onanga nani?*
O.   *Nani.*
L.   *Nani no injo.*
O.   *Nani.*
L.   *E ho! e ovava ovava ovava kwenduni nani. Então sempre kwendano.*
O.   *Mm! Mm!*

Translation:

O.   Going to the house in the land of the black men?
L.   Oh! The black man, hm, walking... the house always less.
O.   Yes! Of course. But what I want to say is: walking in the country for the black man, that is...
L.   Aha!
O: Very much of the black man.
L: Òòò! In the country?
O: Yes.
L: In the country always always less for the black man, the black man who walks over the countryside.
O: Ḿḿ
L: He asks little.
O: Speak.
L: Speak.
O: Speak.
L: Little, isn't that right?
O: Speaking little, and in order to go, a letter, many letters, in many cities, that means, that means, I'm afraid.
L: Being afraid, yes.
O: Yes, I am afraid.
L: And does one speak much in the city?
O: Yes indeed.

L: As for myself, I don't! I'm always afraid, always, very much.
O. Very much. But it is...
L: But always in, always in... speak little?
O: Hm! Little, that's how it is. And the woman of the house goes to peel the cassava, and to soak it, (and) to the beans, in order to eat, to the beans.
L: Rather much.
O: Rather much.
L: Very much, sufficiently enough, of beans.
O: Of course. Because...
L: ...she is going.
O: Much cold. Very much cold... the beans, fire!
L: Cold, cold, fire, but the fire is little! Such is it.
O: No, no, go to the water! There is much water.
L: But no. Father.
O: Because the fire is going from there, is it not so?
L: Aá, little fire, there's nothing left for the father to do than walk far, far into the house.
O: Yes, then from there to go away to drink... drink.
L: And few clothes?
O: Few.
L: Few in the house.
O: Few.
L: And it occurs to me and the water, water, water, little going. Thus always going little.
O: Yes, yes.

Note:

The pronunciation by both parties of some African words differs. For example, Otávio Caetano says *vimbundo*, Ms. Maria de Lourdes however says *jimbundo*, Caetano says correctly in Kimbundu *mbambi* (cold), or *ombambi* in Umbundu, while Ms. de Lourdes says *mambi*.

APPENDIX

B. EXCERPTS FROM INTERVIEW WITH URBANO FERNANDO DE LEITE, APPROX. 50, LEADER OF THE "CONGADA" ASSOCIATION IN THE CITY VILA BELA DA SANTÍSSIMA TRINDADE (MATO GROSSO), 2 NOVEMBER 1980

(Tape A 110/II)

(Transcription by Guilherme dos Santos Barbosa)

Text:

"Embaixador de guerra! Rei meu pai mandou chamá."

"Obedeço a chamá, sunumbuka mukasaia!"

Aí o embaxadô sài prèso. Chega lá, ajueia au pé do rei. Aí o embaxadá ranca um papé du bolso i lê: "Aqui trago essa *mukamba* qui manda seo rê morrê di *bamba,* bem sabê qui nêssa casa festeja o glorioso Benedito Santo, o bem qui sào colocado, e a dança qui bem si vê."

Aí o rei fiala assim: "Alevanta embaixador! Que *vilagodi, vilago.*" Aí eli risca a espada (…)

"Secretalo di guerra! *Grano* vai mi *cunjiar* qui *mukamba* so essa!" Ai eli pega o papé i lê: "Meu irmão, rei de Congo, vou remé das *mukamba* (…) tu prometesse qui mandasse a sua filha princesa. Se acaso num mandá, fazê guerra até vencê-lo" (…)

Translation:

"Envoy of war! The king my lord is calling!"
"I obey the call, *sunumbuka mukasaia!*"

Then the envoy is captured. He arrives and kneels before the king. The envoy pulls a paper from his pocket and reads: "I bring herewith this *mukamba* which orders the king his majesty to die from *bamba,* since you know that in this house the glorious Saint Benedict is celebrated, as the wares which are displayed and the dancing which one clearly sees."

Then the king said: "Stand up, enjoy! Was kind of *vilagodi, vilago*." Then he draws his sword (...)

"Envoy of war! *Grano* will *kunjiar* me what kind of *mukamba* these may be?"

Then he takes the paper and reads: "My brother, King of Congo, I will send (?) a (?) *mukamba* (...) You promised, that you would send your daughter, the princess. If you do not send her, then we will do battle until he is conquered." (...)

C. INDEX OF TAPE RECORDINGS

The entire volume of the sound recordings underlying the investigations of this book of our field research in Brazil has been archived up to now in two places: a) in the Phonographic Archive of the Austrian Academy of Sciences in Vienna; b) in the Department of Ethnomusicoology in the Ethnological Museum in Berlin.

In the following index, recordings are listed according to the original tape numbers in chronological order. One recording often contains several items, for example, several consecutive stories told by the same subject, or several successive pieces of music which were taped without turning off the recorder. This can be seen in each case in the remarks under "Contents of the Recording."

The entries start with a code identifying the culture of origin of the recorded tradition. Using this, the scholar can identify at a glance to which African (or European) regional traditions we are relating the specific items. Our sampling from 1974, 1975, 1979 and 1980 can perhaps one day undergo a quantified analysis after expansion through additional field research. This could lead to interesting results in relation to the regional and thematic division of certain African cultural elements within Brazil.

The character appearing before the description of each recording refers to the following:

o	African-Brazilian tradition with historical basis predominantly in Angola/Congo cultural area
x	African-Brazilian tradition with historical basis predominantly in West Nigeria/Dahomey cultural area
+	Luso- or Ibero-Brazilian tradition
−	Possible presence of cultural elements from southeast Africa (Mozambique, Malawi)

Cases where traditions from various African and European origins have merged with each other in Brazil are designated by multiple adjacent characters.

The first character in such a group indicates a certain dominance. "o x" therefore refers to a creative amalgamation of elements from the Angola/Congo area with those from west Nigeria/Dahomey, with dominance of the former. In the same way, "x o" indicates a converse relationship.

The following information is presented in keywords. Complete protocols for the recordings, including transcriptions of African-Brazilian texts by Guilherme dos Santos Barbosa, are archived at the above mentioned locations.

The recordings are listed in the following format:

> Original tape number
> Recording date
> Recording location
> Recording subject
> Character of cultural dependency (see above)

APPENDIX

Recordings by G. Kubik with D. Kachamba, October 1974

L 129/I/2
19 October 1974
Salvador/Bahia
Samba group with drum, *agogô* (double bell) and scraper; song.
o x

L 129/I/3
19 October 1974
Salvador/Bahia
Samba group with trombone.
o x

L 129/I/4
19 October 1974
Salvador/Bahia
berimbau (gourd bow) with *caxixí*, played by Anaildo, approx. 14 years old, vendor of musical bows at the Mercado Modelo.
o x

L 129/I/5
19 October 1974
Salvador/Bahia
Group with *atabaque* (drum), *agogô* (double bell), *berimbau* (gourd bow) and *pandeiro* (tambourine): rehearsal for a Capoeira fighting game.
o x

Recordings by G. Kubik, September/October 1975

A 1/I/1
19 September 1975
Salvador/Bahia
Verbalization of drummed phrases: stressed syllables depict accent-, motion- and sound-structures. "Tamborim" performer: Vicente dos Santos, male, born 1954.
x

A 1/I/2-5
25 September 1975
Salvador/Bahia
Performance of the "berimbau de barriga" (gourd bow) with *caxixí* (woven rattle): Comprehensive exploration of the sound possibilities of the *berimbau*. Performer: Vicente dos Santos.
o x

A 1/I/6-7
28 September 1975
Salvador/Bahia
Analytical recordings of combinations of *berimbau* and *caxixí* phrases. Performer: Vicente dos Santos.
o x

A 1/II/2
28 September 1975
Salvador/Bahia
Vicente dos Santos playing the *berimbau*.
o x

A 2/I/2
8 October 1975
Salvador/Bahia
Tale of "cacimba de baixo,"
told by Vicente dos Santos.
o

A 2/I/3
8 October 1975
Salvador/Bahia
Tale of a disloyal woman, told
by Vicente dos Santos.
o

A 2/I/4
8 October 1975
Salvador/Bahia
Tale about *sapo* (the toad) going to
a festival of the animals in Heaven,
told by Vicente dos Santos.
o x

A 2/I/5
8 October 1975
Salvador/Bahia
Tale about *cágado* (the mud turtle),
told by Vicente dos Santos.
o x

A 2/I/5
8 October 1975
Salvador/Bahia
Song about "Janaína," the
mythical waterbound female
figure (torso of a young woman, lower body of a fish), sung
by Vicente dos Santos.
x

A 2/I/7
8 October 1975
Salvador/Bahia
How to beat the *atabaques*
(drums) to the above song.
Vicente dos Santos.
x

A 2/I/8
8 October 1975
Salvador/Bahia
Two songs from Umbanda religious practices, Vicente dos Santos.
x

A 2/I/9
8 October 1975
Salvador/Bahia
Riddles. Vicente dos Santos.
x o +

A 2/I/10-11
12 October 1975
Itapoã (a suburb of Salvador/Bahia)
Samba group with *bombo* and
timbal drums, *cuica* friction
drum, *pandeiro* (tambourine),
reco-reco (scraper) and *agogô*
(double bell), recorded in the
garden of the Juvenál pub.
o

A 2/I/12
12 October 1975
Itapoã (a suburb of Salvador/Bahia)
Another *samba* group, same
location, similar ensemble.
o

A 2/I/13
12 October 1975
Itapoã (a suburb of Salvador/Bahia)
Street *samba* group, similar ensemble.
o

A 2/I/14
12 October 1975
Itapoã (a suburb of Salvador/Bahia)
Another street *samba* group with large drum and *agogô* (Yorùbá bell).
o x

A 2/I/15
12 October 1975
Itapoã (a suburb of Salvador/Bahia)
Another street *samba* group with *agogô* and bass drum.
x o

Recordings by G. Kubik, April/May 1979

A 63/I/1
10 April 1979
Cafundó (near Salto de Pirapora, the state of São Paulo)
Recording of conversations (in local Portuguese) in the house of Ms. Maria de Lourdes (approx. 40 years old) with children and visitors.
+

A 63/I/2
10 April 1979
Cafundó (near Salto de Pirapora, the state of São Paulo)
Popular song (Portuguese), sung by the girls Ana Lúcia (about 14) and Alzira (about 16).
+

A 63/I/3
10 April 1979
Cafundó (near Salto de Pirapora, the state of São Paulo)
The boy Gildo (about 14) coaxes rhythmic calls from a chicken.
+

A 63/I/4
10 April 1979
Cafundó (near Salto de Pirapora, the state of São Paulo)
Another popular song (Portuguese) by the girls Ana Lúcia and Alzira.
+

A 63/I/5
10 April 1979
Cafundó (near Salto de Pirapora, the state of São Paulo)
Spoken game between the girls Ana Lúcia and Alzira.
+ o

A 63/I/6
10 April 1979
Cafundó (near Salto de Pirapora, the state of São Paulo)
"A língua africana" (the African language) spoken by Otávio Caetano, about 60 years old, the leader of Cafundó village.
o

A 63/I/7
10 April 1979
Cafundó (near Salto de Pirapora, the state of São Paulo)
Conversation in the "African language" between Otávio Caetano and Jovenil Norberto Rosa (male, about 19-20 years old).
o

A 63/I/8
11 April 1979
Cafundó (near Salto de Pirapora, the state of São Paulo)
Walking song (Portuguese) by Marina (female, about 18-19 years old).
+

A 63/I/9
11 April 1979
Cafundó (near Salto de Pirapora, the state of São Paulo)
Popular song (Portuguese), sung by Alzira.
+

A 63/I/10
11 April 1979
Cafundó (near Salto de Pirapora, the state of São Paulo)
Popular song (Portuguese), sung by Ana Lúcia and Alzira.
+

A 63/I/11
11 April 1979
Cafundó (near Salto de Pirapora, the state of São Paulo)
Popular song (Portuguese), sung by Ana Lúcia and Alzira.
+

A 63/I/12
11 April 1979
Cafundó (near Salto de Pirapora, the state of São Paulo)
Recitative and popular song, presented by Ana Lúcia and Alzira.
+

A 63/I/13
12 April 1979
Cafundó (near Salto de Pirapora, the state of São Paulo)
Song of "Oricongo," from the time of slavery, sung by Otávio Caetano; supplementary remarks: Silvino Pires (male, approx. 70 years old).
o

A 63/I/14
12 April 1979
Cafundó (near Salto de Pirapora, the state of São Paulo)
Short talk about the *tambú* drum and *samba* with Silvino.
o

APPENDIX

A 63/I/15
12 April 1979
Cafundó (near Salto de Pirapora, the state of São Paulo)
Inquiry as to whether the word *kasimba* is known here. Negative response.
o

A 63/II/1
13 April 1979
Cafundó (near Salto de Pirapora, the state of São Paulo)
Song from a hymnbook (Portuguese) sung by Valderez (female, about 30 years old) and Maria de Lourdes Rosa de Almeida (about 35 years old).
+

A 63/II/2
13 April 1979
Cafundó (near Salto de Pirapora, the state of São Paulo)
Maria de Lourdes speaking the "African language" in the presence of children.
o

A 63/II/3
13 April 1979
Cafundó (near Salto de Pirapora, the state of São Paulo)
Dialogue between Otávio Caetano and Maria de Lourdes in the "African language."
o

A 63/II/5
13 April 1979
Cafundó (near Salto de Pirapora, the state of São Paulo)
Otávio Caetano sings "early music" (*música antiga*).
o +

A 63/II/6
13 April 1979
Cafundó (near Salto de Pirapora, the state of São Paulo)
Another song from the hymnbook, sung by Ms. Valderez and Ms. Maria de Lourdes.
+ o

A 63/II/7-10 and A 64/I/1-8, II/1-2
13 April 1979
Cafundó (near Salto de Pirapora, the state of São Paulo)
Dance evening with the accordion player Virginio Pedro da Silva (approx. 40 years old) from Pernambuco; his son Carlinhos (about 14) and inhabitants of Cafundó. This *samba* is contingent on the music of Pernambuco. Instrumentation: accordion, triangle, guitar, *bombo* drum.
o

A 64/II/3
15 April 1979
Cafundó (near Salto de Pirapora, the state of São Paulo)
Conversation with Emiliano Jovino de Almeida (the leader of the Caxambu residents driven out by the landowner) on the site of the former settlement. Information about the history of the place and the region, about *samba*, *tambu* drums, Umbanda, serpent tales, etc.
o

A 64/II/4
15 April 1979
Cafundó (near Salto de Pirapora, the state of São Paulo)
Continuation of the conversation with Emiliano in his house in Salto de Pirapora, where he has lived since the expulsion. (About playing the *tambú*, with a demonstration, and about words in the "African language," etc).
o

A 64/II/5 and A 65/I/1
15 April 1979
Cafundó
Oral sound effects and motion rhythms during rice-winnowing. Performer: Silvino Pires (male, about 70 years old).
o

A 65/I/2-4
15 April 1979
Cafundó
"Nosso Samba" (our *samba*), meaning the *samba* of Cafundó, performed by Otávio Caetano, Noel Rosa de Almeida (approx. 40 years old) and Jovenil (approx. 19-20 years old).
o

A 65/I/5
16 April 1979
Cafundó
Jovenil Norberto Rosa (approx. 19-20 years old) drumming with index, middle and ring fingers on a metal rattle (*xakwayo*) made from the top of a watering can.
o

A 65/I/6
16 April 1979
Cafundó
Rumba-style rhythm played by Carlinhos, approx. 14 years old, (triangle) with Jovenil (rattle)—the 8-mm audio film is available.
o

A 65/I/7
16 April 1979
Cafundó
Forró beat rhythm played by Carlinhos (triangle)—the 8-mm audio film is available.
o

A 65/I/8
16 April 1979
Cafundó
Repeat of the *rumba*-style rhythm by Carlinhos.
o

A 65/II/1
26 April 1979
São Paulo
berimbau (gourd bow) performance by visiting Bahian Vicente dos Santos (born 1954) in the framework of my presentation at USP.
o

A 65/II/2 and A 66/I/1
29 April 1979
Capivari (the state of São Paulo)
Interview with *batuque* player and association head Sr. Benedito Caxias (male, 82 years old).
o -

A 66/I/2
29 April 1979
Capivari (the state of São Paulo)
Drum rehearsal in preparation for a *batuque*.
o -

A 66/I/3-4
29 April 1979
Capivari (the state of São Paulo)
Drum tuning.
o -

A 66/I/5
29 April 1979
Capivari (the state of São Paulo)
Continuation of tuning, then phrases for "quinjenge," *tambu*.
o -

A 66/I/6
29 April 1979
Capivari (the state of São Paulo)
Batuque rhythms played by Benedito Caxias and ensemble with "quinjenge," *tambú* and *matraca* (drumsticks) as well as *guaiá* (double cone rattle).
o -

A 66/I/7-9
29 April 1979
Capivari (the state of São Paulo)
Solo songs sung by Caxias.
o +

A 66/I/10
29 April 1979
Capivari (the state of São Paulo)
Solo song by "Dito Cabeçada," (male, about 40 years old).
o +

A 66/I/11
29 April 1979
Capivari (the state of São Paulo)
Solo song by Caxias (repeat).
o +

A 66/I/12
29 April 1979
Capivari (the state of São Paulo)
Solo song by "Dito Cabeçada."
o +

A 66/I/13-14
29 April 1979
Capivari (the state of São Paulo)
Songs of an Umbanda association from Vila Maria Alice in Paraná (south Brazil) sung by a visitor, Sr. Aparecido Morato, about 32 years old. These are songs for the "orixá" (Yorùbá divinities).
x

A 66/I/15-17
29 April 1979
Capivari (the state of São Paulo)
Repetition of a solo song by Caxias; and two additional songs.
o +

A 66/II/1
29 April 1979
Capivari (the state of São Paulo)
Another song from an Umbanda association, sung for an "orixá" by Aparecido Morato.
x

A 66/II/2-3
29 April 1979
Capivari (the state of São Paulo)
More solo songs by Caxias.
o +

A 66/II/4
30 April 1979
Cafundó (the state of São Paulo)
Interview with Ms. Benedita Pires (born 1907) about her grandfather, who was abducted from Congo as a 12-year-old, with a song in Kikoongo which she remembers.
o

A 66/II/5-6
6 May 1979
Vargem do Cural (in the area of Diamantina, Minas Gerais)
Two songs sung by Ms. Patrousina (approx. 50 years old).
+

A 66/II/7
6 May 1979
Vargem do Cural (in the area of Diamantina, Minas Gerais)
Song by Julia Máximo (female, approx. 50 years old).
+

A 66/II/8-10
6 May 1979
En route to the adjacent village Quartel do Indayá
Songs sung by Vicente Hilário dos Santos (female, approx. 13 years old).
+

APPENDIX

A 66/II/11
6 May 1979
Mocambo-type settlement (approx. 1 kilometer from Quartel do Indayá, area of Diamantina, Minas Gerais) Recording of conversation fragments, noises (tape recorder left running).
o

A 66/II/12-13
6 May 1979
Another settlement (approx. 3 kilometers from Quartel ...) Interview with Manoel de Jesus Pacheco (male, about 70 years old).
o

A 66/II/14-16 and A 67/I/1-7
6 May 1979
Quartel do Indayá
Recordings of *visungo* (songs), partially in Portuguese language, partially in "Banguëla" (pronounced *bangwela*) language from Angola, accompanied by a *caixa* (march drum). Most important singer and subject: Sr. Cecilio Assunção Bela Guarda (approx. 60 years old). Also included is an interview about the "língua banguëla."
o +

A 67/II/1
11 May 1979
São Paulo
Recording of instruction and exercises in the Capoeira school, *Centro de Capoeira Ilha De Maré*, headed up by a Bahian, Mestre Paulo Gomes.
o +

A 68/I/1 and II/1
12 May 1979
São Paulo
Recording of a religious event in the Umbanda community *Tenda Espiritual de Umbanda, Justiça de Xangô*.
o x +

Recordings by G. Kubik, Moya A. Malamusi and D. Kachamba, September/November 1980

A 107/I/1-3
23 September 1980
Brasilia (Galpãozinho)
Recordings at the *Clube do Samba de Brasilia*. Ensemble: Carlos Elias with singer Vanja. Style: Samba-Carioca (Rio de Janeiro).
o +

A 107/I/4-5
23 September 1980
Brasilia (Galpãozinho)
Same location. Ensemble: Unidos do Cruzeiro (Tropical).
o +

A 107/I/1-3
23 September 1980
Brasilia (Galpãozinho)
Recordings at the *Clube do Samba de Brasilia*. Ensemble: Carlos Elias with singer Vanja. Style: Samba-Carioca (Rio de Janeiro).
o +

A 107/I/4-5
23 September 1980
Brasilia (Galpãozinho)
Same location. Ensemble: Unidos do Cruzeiro (Tropical)
o +

A 107/I/6
23 September 1980
Brasilia (Galpãozinho)
Paying respect to Waldir Azevedo, a famous deceased *cavaquinho* player.
o +

A 107/I/7-8
23 September 1980
Brasilia (Galpãozinho)
Ensemble: Julinho "Samba Sincopado."
o +

A 107/I/9
23 September 1980
Brasilia (Galpãozinho)
Ensemble: Fina Flôr. The singer was the founder of the Clube do Samba of Brasilia.
o +

A 107/II/1
29 September 1980
Salvador/Bahia
Repentistas (improvising poets with guitar): Bule-Bule and his friend António Martins (both approx. 35 years old).
+ o

A 107/II/2
29 September 1980
Salvador/Bahia
Boy with *berimbau* (gourd bow).
o

A 107/II/3
29 September 1980
Salvador/Bahia
Boy with *berimbau* playing "Angola," one of the *toques* accompanying Capoeira.
o

A 107/II/4
29 September 1980
Salvador/Bahia
Another boy with *berimbau*.
o

A 107/II/5
29 September 1980
Salvador/Bahia
Gilson dos Santos (male, approx. 16 years old) with *berimbau*.
o

APPENDIX

A 108/I and II
5 October 1980
Recife
Recording of the dance "Xaxado" with accordion, triangle and *pandeiro* (tambourine) by the ensemble Egidio Bezerra from the municipality Bezerros near Recife.
+ o

A 109/I
12 October 1980
Fortaleza
Recording of the Escola de Samba "Girassol" directed by Descartes Marques Gadelha. Instruments: various drums, friction drum (*cuíca*), *cavaquinho, pandeiro,* and *reco-reco.* Recordings of Samba and Forró, a music form from the northeast.
o +

A 110/I/1-10
21 October 1980
Cafundó (near Salto de Pirapora, the state of São Paulo)
Experiment of musical comprehension: Ensemble playing by the musicians from Cafundó (Jovenio on accordion, Laercio on drum, etc.) and Donald Kachamba (guitar). Numerous recordings.
o

A 110/II/11
26 October 1980
Cafundó (near Salto de Pirapora, the state of São Paulo)
Interview with the woman Benedita Pires (born 1907) by Guilherme dos Santos Barbosa about various African words that she remembers.
o

A 110/II/1
2 November 1980
Vila Bela da Santíssima Trindade (Mato Grosso)
Interview with Urbano Fernando de Leite (approx. 50 years old), leader of the Congada ceremonies, about election and installation of a "King of Congo" (contains many Kikoongo words within Portuguese text).
o

A 110/II/2-3
2 November 1980
Vila Bela da Santíssima Trindade (Mato Grosso)
Continuation of interview with some songs (containing Kikoongo words).
o

A 110/II/4-10
2 November 1980
Vila Bela da Santíssima Trindade (Mato Grosso)
Children's games with round dance in the evening (Roda).
+ o

BIBLIOGRAPHY

António de Alva. *Como desmanchar trabalhos de Quimbanda (Mapa Negra)*, Vol. II. Editoria Eco, Rio de Janeiro, 1970.

Amadeu Amaral. *O Dialeto Caipira*. São Paulo, 1976.

Julieta de Andrade. "Brasileiros do Norte falam 'Lanc-Patuá'," in *D.O. Leitura*, Publiçação Cultural da Imprensa Oficial do Estado, Ano 1, Número 12, São Paulo, maio de 1983, pp. 10-11.

Maynard Araújo. *Cultura popular brasileira*. São Paulo, 1973.

M.L. Rodrigues de Areia. "Estrutura magico-religiosa de uma trilogia tradicional nas populações de Angola," *In Memoriam Jorge Dias*, III, Instituto de Alta Cultura, Junta de Investigações Cientificas do Ultramar, Lisboa, 1974.

M.L. Rodrigues de Areia. *Les symboles divinatoires: Analyse socio-culturelle d'une technique de divination des Cokwe de l'Angola*. Instituto de Antropologia, Universidade de Coimbra, 1985.

Almir das Areias. *O que é Capoeira*. São Paulo, 1983.

Guilherme dos Santos Barbosa. "Cafundó, uma comunidade que corre o risco de dissolução," *Bulletin of the International Committee on Urgent Anthropological and Ethnological Research*, No. 20, 1978, pp. 93-104.

Guilherme dos Santos Barbosa. "Antropologia urgente em Cafundó: Uma comunidade afro brasileira sob pressão externa, Vortrag gehalten beim I.U.A.E.S. Intercongress Amsterdam 22-25 April 1981," *Review of Ethnology*, Vol. 8, No. 11-19, 1982, pp. 138-152.

Guilherme dos Santos Barbosa. *Lamentação das almas: Um aspecto cultural da cidade de Xique-Xique*. (Manuscript)

William Bascom. *The Yoruba of southwestern Nigeria*. London, 1969.

Roger Bastide. *Les religions africaines au Brésil*. Presse Universitaires de France, Paris, 1961.

Gerhard Béhague. "Brazil," in *The New Grove Dictionary of Music and Musicians*. Macmillan, London, 1980.

Ulli Beier. *Das Gesicht der Götter: Wie sich die Yoruba-Götter durch ihre Priester mani-*

festieren. Eine Photoaustellung. Bayreuth. Iwalewa- Haus, Februar 1982.

Hermilo Borba Filho. *Apresentação do Bumba-meu-boi.* Recife, Imprensa Universitária, 1966.

Lourenço Braga. *Umbanda é magia branca, Quimbanda magia negra.* Edições Spiker, Rio de Janeiro, 1961.

Vemey Lovett Cameron. *Across Africa.* London, 1885.

Edison Carneiro. *Negros Bantus.* Rio de Janeiro, 1937.

Edison Carneiro. *Candomblés da Bahia.* Secretaria da Educação e Saúde, 1948.

Antônio Carreira. *O tráfico português de escravos na costa oriental africana nos começos do século XIX* (Estudo de um caso). Estudos de Antropologia Cultural No. 12, Lisboa, 1979.

Henrique Augusto Dias de Carvalho. *Expedição Portuguesa ao Muatiânvua: Ethnographia e história tradicional dos povos da Lunda.* Imprensa Nacional, Lisboa, 1890.

José Jorge de Carvalho. *Ritual and music of the Sango cults of Recife, Brazil.* Ph.D. Dissertation, Queen's University, Belfast, 1984.

Luis da Câmara Cascudo. *Dicionário do Folclore Brasileiro,* Rio de Janeiro, 1954.

Ricardo Cassiano. *Marcha para Oeste.* José Olympio, Rio de Janeiro, 1940.

Lieutenant Chamberlain. *Views and costumes of the city and neighbourhood of Rio de Janeiro,* Brazil, 1819-1820. London, 1822.

Gérard Ciparisse. Muziek van de Mpangu, West-Kongo. *Schallplatte Nr. 7,* Musée Royal de l'Afrique Centrale, Tervuren, 1973.

Cristina Argenton Colonelli. "Bibliografia de Folclore Brasileiro," in *Introdução ao estudo da Antropologia no Brasil,* 2nd volume, Encontro Internacional de Estudos Brasileiros, São Paulo, 1971, pp. 122-329

Gilka Corrêa de Oliveira. "Bumba-meu-Boi," Museu do Homen do Nordeste, Recife (n.d.).

Philip D. Curtin. *The Atlantic slave trade: A Census.* The University of Wisconsin Press, Madison, 1969 [1975].

Basil Davidson. *Black Mother: Africa and the Atlantic slave trade.* Pélican, London, 1980

BIBLIOGRAPHY

Alfons M. Dauer. *"Geschichte und Systeme des europäischen Sklavenhandels,"* Jazzforschung – Jazz research, 10, 1978.

Jean-Baptiste Debret. Voyage pittoresque et historique au Brésil, ou Séjour d'un artiste français au Brésil depuis 1816 jusqu'en 1831 inclusivement. Paris, 1834.

Thomas Ewbank. *Life in Brazil: or a journey to the land of the cocoa and the palm.* New York, Harper and Bros., 1856.

Cândido Emanuel Félix. *A cartilha da Umbanda.* Editõra Eco, Rio de Janeiro, 1972.

Alexandre Rodrigues Ferreira. Viagem filosófica pelas Capitanias do *Grão* Pará, Rio Negro, Mato Grosso e Cuiabá, *1783-1792. Rio de Janeiro, 1971-1974.*

Horst H. Figge. *Beiträge zur Kulturgeschichte Brasiliens unter besonderer Berücksichtigung der Umbanda-Religion und der westafrikanischen Ewe-Sprache.* Dietrich Reimer Verlag, Berlin, 1981.

Gilberto Freyre. *Casa Grande e Senzala.* Rio de Janiero, José Olympio, 1943.

Grégoire Le Guexmec, José Francisco Valente. *Dicionário Português - Umbundu.* Instituto de Investigação Cientifica de Angola. Luanda, 1972.

Malcolm Guthrie. *Comparative Bantu: An introduction to the Comparative Linguistics and Prehistory of the Bantu Languages.* 4 Vols. Famborough, 1967-71.

Alex Haley. *Roots.* Hutchinson & Co., Ltd., London, 1977.

A. Heine. *Afrikanische Verkehrssprachen.* Schriften zur empirischen Sozialforschung, Bd. 4, Köln, 1968.

Melville J. Herskovits. *The myth of the Negro past.* Boston, 1941.

Melville J. Herskovits. *Pesquisas etnológicas na Bahia: Sociedade brasileira de antropologia e etnologia.* Publicação do Museu do Estado da Bahia, 1942.

Melville J. Herskovits. *Acculturation: The study of culture contact.* J.J. Augustin, New York, 1938.

Walter Hirschberg. "Kulturhistorie und Ethnohistorie," *Mitteilungen zur Kulturkunde,* Bd. 1, 1966.

Instituto Nacional de Línguas. *Histórico sobre a criação dos alfabetos em línguas nacionais.* Instituto Nacional do Livro e do Disco, Luanda, 1980.

Harry Johnston. *The Negro in the New World.* Macmillan Co., New York, 1910.

Arthur M. Jones. "The Mganda dance," *African Studies*, December, 1945.

Luka Katiapa Kangamba, Robert Chilemu, Benjamine Kasavi. "Chisem- wa cha vwangana vwa Luchazi - The custom of Luchazi chieftainship," *Review of Ethnology*, Vol. 4, No. 18-19, 1976.

Kazadi wa Mukuna. *Contribuição Bantu na música popular brasileira.* Global Editora, São Paulo, 1979.

Kazadi wa Mukuna. "Bumba-meu-boi in Maranhão," in. Tiago de Oliveira Pinto (ed.). *Brasilien: Einführung in Musiktraditionen Brasiliens*. B. Schott's Söhne, Mainz, 1986.

R. K. Kent. "Palmares. an African state in Brazil," *The Journal of African History*, 6, 1965 (pp. 161-175). Reprinted in Richard Price (ed.). *Maroon Societies: Rebel slave communities in the Americas*. Anchor Books, New York, 1973

Martin L. Kilson, Robert I. Rotberg. *The African Diaspora: Interpretive Essays*. Harvard University Press, Cambridge, Massachusetts and London, England 1976.

Sigismund W. Koelle. *Polyglotta Africana...* Edited by P. E. H. Hair and D. Dalby. Sierra Leone, 1963 (first edition London, 1854).

Henry Koster. *Travels in Brazil.* Longman, London, 1816 (*Viagems ao Nordeste do Brasil*. Tradução e notas de Luis de Câmara Cascudo, Companhia Editoria Nacional, São Paulo, 1942).

Gerhard Kubik. *Angolan traits in black music, games and dances of Brazil: A study of African cultural extensions overseas*. Estudos de Antropologia Cultural, No. 10, Lisboa, 1979.

Gerhard Kubik. "African and European transculturation in the field of expressive culture," in *Dialog Westeuropa - Schwarzafrika: Inventar und Analyse der gegenseitigen Beziehungen* (Ed. Otto Molden), Wien, 1979b.

Gerhard Kubik. *Mukanda na makisi* - Circumcision school and masks – Beschneidungsschule und Masken, Record MC 11, Museum für Völkerkunde, Berlin--West, Musikethnologische Abteilung, Berlin, 1981a.

Gerhard Kubik. Review article on "Histórico sobre a criação dos alfabetos em línguas nacionais" (Instituto Nácional de Línguas), Luanda 1980, in *Review of Ethnology*, Vol. 7, Nos. 19-20, 1981b.

Gerhard Kubik. "Erziehungssysteme in ost- und zentralafrikanischen Kulturen

– Forschungsansätze, -methoden und -ergebnisse," *Mitteilungen der Anthropologischen Gesellschaft in Wien,* CXII. Band, Wien, 1982.

Gerhard Kubik. "Afrikanische Musikkulturen in Brasilien," in Tiago de Oliveira Pinto. *Brasilien.* Schott, Mainz, 1986a.

Gerhard Kubik. "Hubert Kponton (1905-1982), Erfinder, Künstler und Begründer eines ethnographischen Privatmuseums in Lomé, Togo," *Archiv für Völkerkunde,* Nr. 40, Museum für Völkerkunde, Wien, 1986b.

Gerhard Kubik. "African graphie systems, with particular referente to the Benue-Congo or 'Bantu' languages zone," *Muntu,* Revue Scientifique et Culturelle du CICIBA, 4-5, année 1986c (Libreville).

Laoye II, Timi of Ede. "Yoruba drums," *Odù.* A Journal of Yoraba and related studies, Vol. 7, 1959, pp. 5-14.

Rossini Tavares de Lima. *Folclore de São Paulo.* Ricordi, São Paulo, 1954.

Rossini Tavares de Lima. *Folguedos populares do Brasil.* Ricordi Brasileira S.A.E.C., São Paulo, 1962.

Oliveira Magno. *Ritual prático de Umbanda.* Editôra Espiritualista. Ltda, Rio de Janeiro, 1961.

Carl Friedrich Phillip von Martius & Johann Baptist von Spix. *Atlas zur Reise in Brasilien* (1817-1820), 4 Bände, München 1823-1831.

Aires da Mata Machado Filho. *O Negro e o Garimpo em Minas Gerais: Coleção Documentos Brasileiros,* 42, Livraria José Olympio Editora, Rio de Janeiro, 1943.

Renato Mendonça. *A influencia africana no Portugués do Brasil.* Companhia Editora Nacional, São Paulo, 1935.

Alan P. Merriam. "Songs of the Ketu cult of Bahia, Brazil," *African Music,* Vol. 1, No. 3, 1956 and Vol. 1, No. 4, 1957.

Domingos Morais. *Os instrumentos musicais e as viagems dos Portugueses.* Instituto de Investigação Cientifica Tropical, Museu de Ethnologia, Lisboa, 1986.

Fernando A. A. Mourão. "La contribution de l'Afrique Bantoue à la formation de la société brésilienne. Une tentative de redefinition méthodologique," Centro de Estudos Africanos, Universidade de São Paulo, 1974a; *África,* USP, São Paulo, 3, 1980, pp. 1-17.

Fernando A. A. Mourão. "Reprise de l'Afrique au Brésil," Communication au

Colloque "Négrítude et Amerique Latine," du 7 au 12 jan- vier 1974, Dakar, Centro de Estudos Africanos, Universidade de São Paulo, 1974b.

Fernando A. A. Mourão. "A contribuição de Gilberto Freyre em *Casa Grande & Senzala* para o estudo da sociedade brasileira: o papel da cultura africana," *Revista de história,* No. 105, São Paulo, 1976, pp. 121-146.

Fernando A. A. Mourão. *A Sociedade Angolana através da Literatura,* Ensaios 38, Editora Atica, São Paulo, 1978.

Jocelyn Murray (Ed.). *Cultural Atlas of África,* Phaidon Press Ltd., Oxford, 1981.

Maria Mutti. *Maculêlê.* Salvador 1978.

Jerome O Ojo. *Yoruba customs from Ondo.* Acta Ethnologica et Linguistica, No. 37, Series Africana 10, Wien, 1976.

Fernando Ortiz. *Contrapunteo Cubano dei Tabaco y el Azúcar.* La Habana, 1940.

Renato Ortiz. *A Morte Branca do Feiticeiro Negro.* Petrópolis, 1978.

Emil Pearson. *Ngangela - English Dictionary.* Cuemavaca, Morelos (México), 1970.

Emil Pearson. *People of the aurora.* Beta books, San Diego (U.S.A), 1977.

João Baptista Borges Pereira. "Estudos antropológicos das populações negras na Universidade de São Paulo," *Revista de Antropologia,* USP, São Paulo, Vol. 24, 1981, pp. 63-74.

João Baptista Borges Pereira. "Estudos antropológicos e sociológicos sobre o negro no Brasil – Aspectos históricos e tendências atuais," in *Contribuições à Antropologia em homenagem ao Professor Egon Schaden.* Coleção Museu Paulista, Série Ensaios, vol. 4, São Paulo, 1981, pp. 3-15

Maria Isaura Pereira de Queiroz. "Evolution et création religieuses. les cultes afro-brésiliens," *Díogène,* No. 115, Paris, 1981.

Yeda Pessoa de Castro. "Das línguas africanas ao Português Brasileiro," *Afro-Asia,* No. 14, Salvador, Dezembro de 1983.

Donald Pierson. *Os africanos da Bahia.* Departamento de Cultura, São Paulo, 1941.

Donald Pierson. *O candomblé da Bahia,.*Guaíra, Curitiba, 1942.

Tiago de Oliveira Pinto. "Capoeira, das Kampfspiel aus Bahia," in T. O. Pinto (ed.), *Brasilien: Einführung in Musiktraditionen Brasiliens,* Mainz, 1986a.

Tiago de Oliveira Pinto. "Candomblé," in T. O. Pinto (Ed.), *Brasilien: Einführung in*

Musiktraditionen Brasiliens" Mainz, 1986b.

Tiago de Oliveira Pinto. "Musik im Candomblé aus Bahia," in Programmheft *Brasilien,* Internationales Institut f. Vergleichende Musikstudien, Berlin, 1986c.

Tiago de Oliveira Pinto. "Historische afro-brasüianische Siedlungsformen zwischen Auflösung und Anpassung in Brasiliens gegenwärtiger sozio- ökonomischer Entwicklung," in *Review of Ethnology,* Vol. 10, No, 1- 13, pp. 83-85.

Tiago de Oliveira Pinto. *Capoeira, Samba, Candomblé. Afro-brasi Uanische Musik im Recôncavo, Bahia.* Publikationen des Museums für Völkerkunde, Berlin, Neue Folge Nr. 52, Berlin, 1991.

Dorothy B. Porter. *Afro-Brazäiana, a working bibliography,* G. K. Hall & Co., Boston, Mass., 1978

Manoel Querino. *A Bahia de Outr'ora.* Vultos e Fatos Populares. Salvador, 1916

Manuel Querino. *A arte culinária na Bahia.* Livraria Progresso, Salvador, 1954

Arthur Ramos. *As culturas negras no novo mundo.* Civilização Brasileira, Rio de Janeiro, 1937

Arthur Ramos.*Aculturação negra no Brasil.* Cia. ed. Nacional, São Paulo, 1942

T. O. Ranger. *Dance and society in eastern Africa 1890-1970. The Beni Ngoma.* Heinemann Educational Books Ltd., London, 1975

Waldeloir Rego. *Capoeira Angola.* Ensaio sócio-etnográfico. Editora Itapu, Coleção Baiana, Rio de Janeiro, 1968

Joaquim Ribeiro. *Folclore baiano,* MEC, Rio de Janeiro, 1956

M. J. Borges Ribeiro. *A dança de Moçambique.* ed. Ricordi, São Paulo, 1960

Nina Rodrigues. *Os africanos no Brasil,* Ciá. ed. Nacional, São Paulo, 1945

E. C. Rowlands. *Yoruba. A complete working course: Teach yourself books.* Hodder and Stoughton, London, 1969

Johann Moritz Rugendas. *Malerische Reise in Brasilien.* Paris, 1835.

Mose Kaputungu Sangambo. *The history of the Luvale people and their chieftainship* (ed. by Art Hansen and R. J. Papstein) Africa Institute for Applied Research, Los Angeles, 1979.

Stuart B. Schwartz. "The Mocambo. slave resistance in colonial Bahia," *Journal of Social History*, Vol. 3, 1970 (pp. 313-333). Reprinted in. Richard Price (ed.). *Maroon Societies: Rebel slave communities in the Americas.* Anchor Books, New York, 1973.

Société Française d'Histoire d'Outre-Mer. *La traite des noirs par VAtlantique: Nouvelles approches.* Bibliothèque d'Histoire d'Outre-Mer, Nouvelle série, Etudes 4, Paris, 1976.

William C. Sturtevant. "Anthropology, history and ethnohistory," *Ethnohistory*, Vol. 13, No. 1-2, 1966.

Robert Farris Thompson. *Flash of the Spirit: African and Afro-American Art and Philosophy.* Vintage Books, New York, 1984.

Jan Vansina. *Oral tradition: A study of historical methodology.* London, 1965.

Pierre Verger. "Yoruba influences in Brazil," *Odù* - Journal of Yoruba and Related Studies (Ibadan), No. 1, January, 1955.

Pierre Verger. *Flux et reflux de la traite des nègres entre le golfe de Bénin et Bahia de Todos os Santos du dix-septième au dix-neuvième siècle.* Mouton, Paris, 1968.

Pierre Verger. *Notes sur le culte des Orisa et Vodun,* Ifan, Dakar, 1975.

Pierre Fatumbi Verger. *Orixás,* São Paulo, 1981.

Carlos Vogt, Peter Fry y Maurizio Gnerre. "Las lenguas secretas de Cafundó," *Ponto de Vista,* 1980, pp. 26-32.

Carlos Vogt e Peter Fry. "Ditos e feitos da Falange Africana do Cafundó e da Calunga de Patrocínio (ou de como fazer falando)," *Revista de Antropologia,* Vol. 26, 1983, pp. 65-92.

Dietrich Westermann. *Wörterbuch der Ewe-Sprache.* Berlin, 1905-1906.

Dietrich Westermann. *Grammatik der Ewe-Sprache.* Berlin, 1907.

D. Westermann and Ida C. Ward. *Practical Phonetics for students of African languages.* International African Institute, London, 1933 [1966].

Heinz Wieschhoff. Die afrikanischen Trommeln und ihre amserafrikani- schen Beziehungen. *Stuttgart, Strecker & Schröder, 1933.*

NOTES

1. Cf. the orthographies for the six national languages of Angola, Kikoongo, Kimbundu, Umbundu, Mbunda, Cokwe and Nyaneka—the Instituto Nacional de Línguas 1980.

2. Cf. Herskovits's basic concepts of "retention," "selection" and "reinterpretation."

3. See Chamberlain 1822, Debret 1834, Johnston 1910, and Rugendas 1835.

4. Cf. Debret 1834, Rugendas 1835, Ramos 1937 and other authors.

5. Henry Koster 1816, 505 (Portuguese translation 1942).

6. Koster, 508.

7. Mourão 1974a, 6-7

8. Verger 1968, 10-11

9. Cf. contemporary reports by Martius & J. B. von Spix, 1817-1820, Lieutenant Chamberlain 1822, Jean-Baptiste Debret 1834, Johann Moritz Rugendas 1835, Thomas Ewbank 1856 and others.

10. Koelle 1854; new edition with an introduction by P. E. H. Hair and D. Dalby 1963.

11. Cf. maps in Curtin 1975, 253-257.

12. Interview, January 1970, Lomé, Togo.

13. Interview with Hubert Kponton in January 1970, Lomé, Togo.

14. Notes from a presentation by Marcelina Gomes in Luanda, Departamento Nacional de Folclore, 17 February 1982.

15. Kangamba 1976, 151 (translation from Luchazi by G. Kubik).

16. See recordings from the suburb Itapoã A 2/I/10-15, 1975.

17. Cf. my remarks in Tiago de Oliveira Pinto, 1986a, 131-132.

18. Cf. Kubik in T. de Oliveira Pinto 1986a, 121-129.

19. Cf. my sound recordings from Firmino Lorenço Junior, Luanda, January 1981, Volume 113, Museum für Völkerkunde, Berlin.

20. Cf. Kubik 1979a:17-18 and 1976 on the topic of musical structural evidence.

21. Interview with Mose Yotamu, 3 December 1978.

22. Interview with Mose Yotamu, 3 December 1978.

23. Cf. this song to my recording "Mukanda na makisi," MC 11, Museum für Völkerkunde Berlin, 1981.

24. Cf. Verger, 1968.

25. Just to name a few: Roger Bastide 1961; Edison Carneiro 1948; Melville J. Herskovits 1942; Alan P. Merriam 1956; Donald Pierson 1941, 1942; Manuel Querino 1954; Arthur Ramos 1937; Joachim Ribeiro 1956; Nina Rodrigues 1945; Pierre Verger 1975.

26. See de Oliveira Pinto, ed., 1986a.

27. Cf. the documentary I filmed in collaboration with my African associate Moya A. Malamusi in November 1980, *Rio de Janeiro por olhos africanos* – Rio de Janeiro through African Eyes.

28. Cf. Gilberto Freyre 1943.

29. Rugendas 1835, 10-11, 21.

30. See Guilherme dos Santos Barbosa 1978, 1982.

31. Letter document of 19 May 1981, regarding the possibility of re-settlement of displaced residents of Caxambu, Município de Sarapui.

32. dos Santos Barbosa 1982, 141)

33. Cf. my recording of the working rhythm while winnowing rice, Volumes A 64/II/5 and A 65/I/1, Index.

34. Volume A 64/II/3-4.

35. See chapter III and Appendix.

36. Above all, interviews from June-September 1979 at the Zambia/Angola border, then in Luanda, and in January 1981 a second time in Luanda.

37. The address of whom we received from Professor Rossini Tavares de Lima, Director of the Museu de Folclore, São Paulo.

38. See transcriptions from film, no. 20, Capivari, 29 April 1979, in Kubik 1986a.

39. This drum carries the catalogue number A0-183 (cf. Kubik 1986a:138.

40. Field recordings Kubik, Angola 1965; LP "Humbi en Handa – Angola," No. 9, Musée Royal de l'Afrique Centrale, Tervuren 1973.

41. Cf. the LP by Gérard Ciparisse "Muziek van de Mpangu," no. 5, Musée Royal de l'Afrique Centrale, Tervuren.

42. See photo on page 22 in the liner notes to the record.

43. Letter to author, dated 11 August 1976. Translation from Portuguese by

44. Recording A 2/I/2, 1975.

45. Cf. recordings A 2/I/4 and 5.

46. Field recordings 1965, 1971, Kubik.

47. See A 2/I/3.

48. Estado de São Paulo, Sunday, November 16, 1980

49. Guilherme dos Santos Barbosa got this information during our stay in Vila Bela (communication of 25 May 1981).

50. Cf. A 110/II/1-3, 2 November 1980.

51. A 110/II/4-10, 2 November 1980.

52. Notes from a lecture by Alexandre Nlamba on 19 February 1982 in the Departamento Nacional de Folklore, Luanda, on the occasion of the seminar I held.

53. A. Hauenstein, in a letter to me, dated 20 November 1981. In reference to the terminology of traditional Angolan medicine, see also the publications of M.L. Rodrigues de Areia (1974 and 1985).

54. Cf. Dictionário Português-Umbundu, Le Guennec/Valente 1972, p. 30.

55. Letter of 20 November 1981.

56. Cf. the example Vila Bela in Mato Grosso, above, as well as Guilherme dos Santos Barbosa's almost mystical relationship to rivers, reflecting a more individual perspective.

57. Mata Machado Filho 1943, 56

58. See recordings A 66/II/14-16 and A 67/I/1-7, 6 May 1979.

59. Quoted from a report by Mario Roberto Zágari, in the Estado de Minas, May 25, 1978.

60. See report by Antônio Fernândes in the *Diário do Congresso Nacional*, Secção II. Brasília, 16 May 1973.

61. Cf. tape recordings A 63/I/6-7, A 63/II/3, A 64/II/4, index.

62. See also my review, Kubik 1981b.

63. Recordings volume A 64/II/3-4, 15 April 1979.

64. Tape recording A 66/II/4, 30 April 1979.

65. Cf. dos Santos Barbosa, Intercongress Report 1982.

66. Compare the recording of our interview with Emiliano, volume A 64/II/4, 15 April 1979 in Salto de Pirapora, in which some girls from the city were present and asked exactly this kind of question.

67. Translation from Portuguese by Kwasi Konadu.

68. Information from A. Hauenstein, 20 November 1981.

69. Diary entry 1 November 1980.

70. Cf. the intonation of a word like *jimbundo* in my recording A 63/II/4, transcribed in Appendix A, that is: *jimbúndó*-òó (- - -) with a glissando-like sinking open *o*.

71. Written memorandum, M. Eduardo Dias de Figueiredo, Luanda, 14 January 1981. Translated from Portuguese by Kwasi Konadu.

72. Tape A 63/II/3, transcription in Appendix.

73. Notes of 14 January 1981 in Luanda.

74. Written memorandum by dos Santos Barbosa, 17 May 1981.

75. Note by A. Hauenstein, in a letter of 20 November 1981.

76. Cf. my sound recordings of Vicente dos Santos, Salvador/Bahia on the "tamborim," tape A 1/1/1, 19 September 1975.

77. Cf. Arthur M. Jones 1945, T.O. Ranger 1975.

78. Cf. the *ondyelwa* dance drama of the "boi sagrado" in Huila province, as well as some groups in the "Carnaval de Luanda."

79. Cf. sound recordings of our interview in Vila Bela, A 110/11/1-3, 2 November 1980.

NOTES

80. An 8-mm film documentation is in the possession of an acquaintance of Ms. Kilza Setti, an anthropologist with the Departamento de Ciências Sociais of the University of São Paulo.

81. Rossini Tavares de Lima 1962, 29

82. Letter to me dated 25 February 1982.

83. Corrêa de Oliveira, n.d.

84. Field records Salvador/Bahia, 6 October 1975.

85. Documentário sonoro do folklore brasileiro – no. 3, MEC-DAC CDFB 003, Ministério da Educação e Cultura, Campanha de Defesa do Folclore Brasileiro.

86. Journal, 6 October 1975.

87. Cf. recordings in the Phonographic Archive in Vienna, B 10072, as well as 8-mm film X 1 in the Kubik personal archive.

88. *Viver Bahia*, no. 25, Outubro 1975: 5.

89. Regendas 1835, 26. See also Kubik 1979a, Fig. 11.

90. Cf. *Viver Bahia*, no. 25, Outubro 1975: 5.

91. For more about the musicological aspects, cf. Kubik 1979a: 30 and Oliveira Pinto, 1986a.

92. Cf. Koster, Rugendas, Debret, etc.

93. Cf. Kubik 1979a, 1986a, Tiago de Oliveira Pinto 1986a.

94. Conversation: Munich, 19 April 1987.

95. Translation from Portuguese by Kwasi Konadu.

96. Quote from correspondence: letter to me of 4 May 1977.

97. Mourão 1980, 6-7

98. Cf. for example the film *Bahia la Sainte* by R. Moride, 1950, 30 mins.

99. Cf. the review of the Centro de Estudos Afro-Orientais, Salvador 1984.

100. Cf. Tiago de Oliveira Pinto 1986b, 160.

101. Letter to me of 30 March 1982.

102. See also the Highlife song by Sir Victor Uwaifo: "Guitar Boy and

Mamywater," Philips West African Records, Dancing time no. 8, 420034 PE.

103. Cf. also tape recordings Volume L 129/II/1 and L 131/I/1.

104. Cf. tapes A 66/II/13, 14, A 66/II/1; see index.

105. Cf. D. Braga 1961, Oliveira Magno 1961, António de Alva 1970, Cândido E. Felix 1972.

106. Field notes on an Umbanda event, recorded in São Paulo, of the association *Tenda Espiritual de Umbanda – Justiça de Xangô*, tape A 68/I/1 and II/1, 12 May 1979.

107. Recordings Kubik/Angola 1965, tape 77/II from Sachingangu; Kubik/Zambia 1971, tapes L 1 and L 2, Chikenge; in the Phonographic Archive in Vienna; as well as unpublished films in the Kubik archive; a few photos of an active *kimbanda* from the Kabompo district, N.W. Zambia province, have in the meantime been shown in a touring exhibition of the Ethnomedical Society in Germany and Austria. In addition, cinematographic documentation of an *umbanda* ritual of removing "evil spirits" from a person and produced during the seventies exists in Wila province, southwest Angola, thanks to Ruy Duarte de Carvalho, film *Makumukas*, Televisão Popular de Angola, 1977-78 production.

108. See two of my presentations during the 12th Congress of the International Musicological Society, Berkeley, 21-27 August, on "African Roots of Music in the Americans" (Chairman: Gerard Béhague) and "Ethnography of Musical Performance" (Chairman: John Blacking); cf. also Kubik 1979a: 7-8.

109. cf. my expositions in Chapter III: African Languages Remnants in Brazil)

110. Mourão 1980, 16

111. Cf. reports in *Time*, 14 February 1977 and *Newsweek*, 4 July 1977.

112. See report in *Daily Nation*, Nairobi, 6 December 1979, by Eduardo Gallardo, Rio de Janeiro.

113. Mourão 1980, 1

114. Mourão 1980, 7-8

115. Cf. the example of time-line patterns in Brazil and West Africa, Kubik 1979a, 13-22, 48.

INDEX

A

abolition   7, 35-6
acculturation   151, 154
adaptation   71, 153, 155
African ancestry   70, 151
African-Bahian, oral tradition   41-2
African-Brazilian
    community   1-3, 8-10, 27-8, 39, 44, 46, 49, 52, 69-71, 74, 80, 86
    cultures   30-1, 33, 39, 94, 106, 124, 151, 156-7, 160
    fighting games   105-6, 108-10, 113, 121-2 *see also* capoeira
    kings   98
    religions   8, 33, 123, 125-6, 135-6 *see also* Candomblé
    vocabulary   51, 67, 69, 73, 75-6, 80, 82, 84-6
African colleagues (as researchers)   80-1, 151
African communities   8, 86, 162
African cultural elements   27-30, 33, 39, 45, 49, 67,
    103, 107, 123-4, 151-2, 155-7, 159, 163-4
African descendants   2, 29, 39, 41-3, 46, 49, 69, 82, 113-14, 138
African diaspora   93, 126, 151-2, 156-7, 159-60, 164
African ethnicities   4, 10 *see also* ethnic groups
African languages   10, 39-42, 67-76, 78-9, 81, 84-5, 92, 141
African perspectives   14, 30, 159, 165
agogô   132-3
altar   96, 132-3
Amerindian chief   101
Amerindian healer   101-2
Amerindian languages   67, 76, 85, 113
Amparo plantation   95-6
ancestors   2, 12, 15, 37, 39, 46, 51, 73, 77-9, 81, 84-5, 92, 162, 165
andalu   77-8, 83
Anecho   15
Angola
    a brincar de   108, 110

central   12, 16
east   5, 16, 24, 32, 41, 50-1, 54, 61, 138, 148
languages of   46-7, 70, 112, 114, 139
north   5, 40, 50, 77, 94, 98
northwest   61, 83
southeast   114, 138
southern   83
southwest   15-16, 40, 99-100, 118-19, 138, 147
Angola area/region   9-11, 28, 32, 36, 40, 63, 83, 94
Angola Candomblé   134 *see also* Candomblé
Angola trade   12
Angolan, peoples   16, 32, 37-8, 76, 93, 105, 107, 110-12, 138, 141, 143
Angolan bows   111 *see also* berimbau
Angolan cultures   28, 50, 143
Angolan descendants   37, 76, 109, 112, 139, 141-2, 166
Angolan *folguedo*   105
Angolan history   46
Angolan medicine   138, 141
Angolan tradition in Brazil   108, 110, 138
associations   93, 108, 124, 135

B

Bahia   1-2, 5, 8-10, 27-9, 33-4, 41-2, 56-7, 69, 106, 109-10, 112, 122-4, 127, 130-1, 133-5
Bahian sugar cane region   30
Bairro   29, 36-8, 58, 76, 88-9
Banguëla language   51, 63, 75
Bantu languages   31-2, 38, 71, 73-4, 77, 87, 114, 136, 143
Bantu regions of Africa   10
bàtá (drum)   34
batuque (dance)   29-30, 39
Belo Horizonte   46, 48, 52-3
Benguela   4-6, 11-12, 28, 54, 83
berimbau   108, 110, 112
black healer *see* kimbanda
boi (bull)   58, 99-100, 102, 104-5, 117 *see also* Bumba-meu-boi
borrowings   45, 67-8, 71, 114, 153

bow   112 *see also* berimbau
Brazil
    coast   1, 46
    colonial   91, 104, 140, 142
    eastern   1, 3
    nineteenth century   40, 69
    northern   68
    rural   105
    southern   10, 123, 136
Brazilian authors   31, 51, 114
Brazilian *folguedos*   29, 92-4, 98-100, 103, 105, 124
Brazilian language   2, 31, 67-71, 139
Brazilian literature   47, 75, 113
Brazilian *maculelê*   32, 106
Brazilian slave traders   15
Brazilian Umbanda   137, 143 *see also* Umbanda
Brazilians of European ancestry   70, 138, 155
Bumba-meu-boi   92, 98-100, 103-5, 117
burials   52, 165-6

C

Cafundó
    inhabitants   38, 68, 76-82, 84, 89, 165
    language of   85
    village of   29, 36-9, 43, 58, 61, 68-9, 71, 73, 76-81, 83-6, 88-9, 165-6
    vocabulary   39, 58, 68, 75-7, 81-4, 86-8
cágado (turtle)   41
Candomblé   27, 34, 69, 123-5, 127-31, 133, 146
    drums   134-5
Capoeira   94, 105, 108-11, 113-15, 120-1
capoeiristas (capoeira practitioners)   106, 111, 121-2
Catholic Church   95-8, 124-5
Caxambu   29, 37, 39, 69, 76, 85, 165-6
Caxias   39, 135-6
caxixi (woven rattle)   112-13
Ceará   99
Central Africa   2, 10, 12, 16, 72, 107, 161

ceremonies   34, 45, 96, 99
Chapada (town)   48-9, 51, 75
chiefs   13-14, 16, 47
chinamwali   165
cities   8, 17, 27, 29, 33-7, 39, 44, 46, 48, 111, 123, 126, 131, 152
civilizations   79-80, 124
class, upper   69, 103-4
cloth   13
coconut trees   51
coffee   49-50, 70
conflict   71, 102-3
Congada   29, 45, 92, 94-5, 97-9, 124, 157
Congo   2, 4-7, 9-12, 14, 27-8, 31, 40, 45, 61, 77, 94-5, 97, 112, 134, 157-8
   descendants in Brazil   94-5
   king of   94, 97
cord-and-peg tension   133-4
creolization   68, 152
Cuabo   11-12
cultural contact   68, 125, 152, 154, 159
cultural elements   9, 28-9, 136, 156, 160
culture traits   160-2

D

Dahomey   2, 5, 8-9, 11, 28, 112, 126, 134-5, 158
dance   8, 29-30, 32, 45, 52, 98, 101, 104-5, 110, 125, 133
   dramas   91-2, 97-8, 104
Diamantina   48-9, 52
divergence   67, 160
Dona Benedita Pires Pedroso   77-8
drummers   121, 132
drums   39-40, 88, 92, 94-5, 106-7, 109, 121, 125, 131-5, 162-3

E

engenhos (sugar mills)   4
enslaved Africans   1, 5, 8-11, 15-16, 19, 22, 33, 36-

7, 44, 49, 72, 84, 97, 102-5, 113-14
  freed   11, 47
  newly-arrived   25, 86, 128
  origin of   2, 72
enslaved Pai Francisco   100-2, 104
ethnic groups   5, 11-12, 31, 54, 75, 83
European cultures   152
European languages   72, 141
European travelers in Central Angola   73
Europeans   14-15, 17, 138, 156, 159, 164
evil magic   47, 139-43
Ewe   2, 28, 112, 126-7, 134-5
Exu   129

F

Festa do Congo   94
Fon   2, 11, 28, 126-7
French-speaking West Africa   132, 142

G

Gegê   2, 4, 127, 134
Ghana   9, 134-5
gold mines   44
Guaporé River   29, 42, 44-6
guns   13-14

H

harbors   9-10
healers, traditional   136-7, 139-42
Huíla   5, 15, 83, 99, 108, 118-19, 147

I

-identity 74, 76, 87, 101, 127, 135
Iemanjà 131
ifumbe 82
Ilhabela 94
Indaiá 29, 48-51, 62-4

J

Janaina 124, 131-2, 144
Johann Moritz Rugendas 1, 3, 24-5, 34, 54-5, 98, 109, 121

K

Kachamba, Donald 41, 71, 81, 116, 164
kafombe 82
kambelela 78
kapwera 114
kasimba 41
Kazadi wa Mukuna 76, 98, 100, 103, 164
kifumbe 82
Kikoongo 39, 45, 47, 71, 74-7, 86, 94
kilombo 46
kimbanda 136-7, 139, 141-2, 147
Kimbundu language 5, 31, 39, 46-7, 51, 71-2, 74-7, 82-3, 109, 136
Kingdom of Kôngo 5, 94, 97, 99, 137
kinjenge 39-40
Koster, Henry 5, 94, 98
Kponton, Hubert 15, 20-1
kulima 74-6
kung-fu 106
kusamba 31-2
Kwanza River 43

L

lamellophones   161
languages   7, 10, 16, 31-2, 39, 42, 47, 51, 67-9, 71-3, 75-6, 78-80, 83-6, 136-7, 152-3
   common   12, 69, 72
   contact   68-70
   foreign   67-9, 153
   indigenous   68, 72-3, 86
   liturgical   33, 125
   secret   68, 73, 80
lé   132-3, 135
leader (of Cafundó)   37, 39, 81, 88, 116, 131
Lima   41, 92, 94, 96
língua Africana   39, 76
Lomé (Togo)   15, 20-1
Luanda   1, 12, 16, 18, 31-2, 47, 75-6, 82-3, 86
Lubalo   11-12
Luso-Brazilian perspective   80, 136
Luso-Brazilian world   81, 136, 139
Luso-Brazilians   27, 39, 69, 71, 87, 103, 138, 141-2
Luvale in East Angola   12, 14, 32, 38-9, 84

M

maculelê   94, 105-9, 113, 161
magic   3, 101-4, 136, 139-42
Makwa   11-12
Malawi   2, 11, 71-2, 92
Mami Wata   131-2
Manding   3-4
mandingueiros   3
Maranhão   3, 28, 99-100
marujada   93-4
matako   86
Mato Grosso   3, 28-9, 43-4, 65, 94, 116
medicines   13, 104, 141
memories   97, 104-5, 108, 165

Milho Verde   51-2
Mina   4, 6-7, 9, 52
Minas Gerais   10, 27, 30, 46, 48, 50-3, 62-4, 69, 73, 75, 80, 86
mocambos   29, 43, 47-8, 50-1
mother tongue   10, 67-70, 72
motif   104-5
Mozambique   2, 4-6, 10-11, 28-9, 40, 61, 70, 72, 92, 160
mphemba   143, 148-9
MPLA Government of Angola   18
Mumbuca   52-3
music   8, 30, 32, 93, 104-5
myth   100-1, 103, 125, 155

N

Nagô   2, 4-5, 9, 27-8, 33-4, 127, 131, 133, 145
neo-African cultural expressions, refined   8
Ngangela group of East Angola   32, 39, 47, 51, 74, 76, 136
Ngangela language group   41, 46, 141
Ngola   11-12
Nigeria   3, 11, 67, 75, 127-8, 130, 132, 134-5
    southwest   8-9, 28
Nyaneka of southwest Angola   104

O

occultism   123, 136, 138
ocimbanda   136-7, 139
oppressors   80, 82-3, 85-6, 102, 124, 153, 155
orixás   8, 127-30, 135
Otavio Caetano, village leader   78, 81, 83
Ouidah   9
Ovimbundu   11-14, 16-17, 47, 73, 82, 108
    slave traders   5, 12
ox   99-104, 117 *see also* boi (bull)
    sacred   99, 104-5
    star   100, 102, 104

Oxalá   124, 128-9
Oyo   11, 126

P

Palmares   47
Pangela   11
patron   100-3, 105
pemba   143
performance   88, 92, 94, 99, 107, 117, 122
Pernambuco   1-3, 5-6, 10, 30, 34, 47, 99
phonology   31, 77, 83
physiognomies   6
Pierre Verger   9
Pirapora   28-9, 36-7, 58, 69, 71, 76-7, 82, 84, 88-9, 165-6
pit trap   38
plantations   4, 36, 86, 109
police   110-11
Polymorphemic expressions in African languages   70
Popó   106-7
Porto Seguro   15, 20
Portugal   2, 9, 84, 93-4, 97, 160
Portuguese language   38, 70-1, 73, 78, 85, 125
    in Brazil   67
Portuguese transcriptions of Yorùbá words   75
practices
    healing   141-2
    traditional healing   139, 141

Q

Quartel   29, 48-51, 62-4
quilombos   29, 46-8, 50, 53, 91, 97
quimbanda   139-40, 142
quinjengue   39-40

R

rattles 31, 40, 112, 132 *see also* caxixi
Rebolos 4-7
Recife 29, 34, 97-8, 117, 123
religion 125, 131, 139-40
retentions 37, 68-9, 151-2
revolts 5, 15, 91, 105
Rio de Janeiro 1-3, 6-7, 10, 24, 28-30, 33-5, 52, 55, 111-13, 123
rites 52, 98, 100, 105, 124, 136, 155
rivers 42-3, 45, 47, 126
rubber 12, 17
ruling Euro-Brazilian classes 140
rum 132-3, 135
rumpi 132-3, 135
Ruy Duarte Carvalho 100

S

salt 13-14, 16
Salto de Pirapora 28-9, 36-7, 58, 69, 71, 76-7, 82, 84, 88-9, 165-6
Salvador (Bahia) 15, 23, 27, 29, 33, 41, 56-7, 106, 111, 120, 122-3, 127, 134, 144-5
samba 30-2, 57
Santíssima Trindade 3, 29, 43, 65, 116
São Francisco 43
São Paulo 2, 28-9, 36, 39, 43-4, 58, 69, 71, 76-7, 80, 88-9, 94, 97, 112, 123
São Tomé 7-8, 15, 160
scepter 95-6
senhor 24, 36, 110, 121, 125
senzalas 29, 36, 86, 109
settlements 29, 37, 46-50, 109
Sierra Leone 10-11
Sigismund W. Koelle 10-12, 72
slave laborers 44
slave trade 6, 9, 13, 15-16, 20, 24, 72, 82
slaveholders 82, 86, 101-3, 109-10, 165
slavery 7, 12, 16, 18, 21, 34-5, 44, 50, 69, 72, 82, 84-5, 91, 105, 111

Songo   11, 39, 83-4
songs   16, 31-2, 34, 38, 41, 48, 51, 75, 77, 93, 133, 135
    religious   135
Southeast Africa   2, 11, 31, 40
spectators   120-1
spirits   43, 125, 138
sticks   32, 40, 106-8, 112-13, 119, 132, 162
    concussion   32, 107-8, 113, 117-18
stories   15-16, 41-2, 100, 102
Swahili   12-13
symbolism   30, 91, 99, 101-2, 126, 133, 141
syncretism   123-5, 127

T

technologies   15, 133, 154
terreiros   127, 130, 150, 155
Togo   11, 15, 20, 112, 126, 134
tonality   31, 42, 81, 83-4
trade   12, 14, 17
trade language   72-3, 84
traditions   9, 15, 29, 31, 92, 98, 107, 161-3
    varied African-Brazilian   111
traits   159, 162
    various African cultural   151
transatlantic slaving   2, 7, 10, 12, 14, 16, 72, 77, 83, 138
transcendental beings   126, 138-9, 143
transfer, morphemic   70
treaties   9, 103

U

Ulli Beier   125-6
Umbanda   40, 135-43, 147, 150
Umbundu   5, 12, 16, 39, 46, 51, 71-5, 77, 81, 83, 86, 136
    words   73, 78
Urban African-Brazilian cultures   29

V

Vicente dos Santos 41-2
Vila Bela 3, 29, 43-6, 65, 116
villages 12-14, 36-8, 43, 46-7, 52, 76, 108-9, 118-19, 149, 166
visitors 46, 77-8, 86
vissungos 48, 51-2, 64, 75
vodu 126-7

W

wanga 140-1
war 13, 97, 111, 160, 162
wax 12, 16-17
West Africa 2, 9, 22, 33, 40, 75-6, 110, 126-8, 132, 134, 156-8
 area of origin 112, 134
white kaolin 143, 149
white magic 139, 141-2
wives 125
women 24, 42, 49-50, 56, 63, 93, 95, 100-2, 124, 131-3, 157

X

Xangô 75, 123-5, 135, 150
Xique-Xique 43

Y

Yao 11-12
Yemanjá 124, 129
Yorùbá 8-9, 11, 27-8, 33, 42, 71-2, 75, 125-7, 130, 133, 135-6, 158
Yorùbá culture 9, 33, 123, 131
Yorùbá language 34, 69, 133
Yorùbá music in Brazil 135
Yorùbá òrìxà 124, 135
Yorùbá people in Brazil 2, 5

Yorùbá religion   27, 124-7, 138
Yorùbá religion to Bahia   128
Yorùbá words in Bahia   75, 135
youths   51, 106-7

Z

Zambia   2, 12, 14, 92, 158

www.ingramcontent.com/pod-product-compliance
Lightning Source LLC
Chambersburg PA
CBHW071157070526
44584CB00019B/2834